RAVENNA EFFECT - THE COUP D'ÉTAT WAS CIVIL

How Versaillism and demagogy turned Brazil unviable

Cacildo Marques

Copyright © 2018 Cacildo Marques - All rights reserved

ISBN: **978-1719187572**

Cover design: Cacildo Marques

With base in the second edition in Portuguese, March 2018.

Marques, Cacildo
Ravenna Effect – The coup d'état was civil/ Cacildo Marques. Maryland.
EpistemeEd , 2018.

108p.
ISBN: **978-1719187572**

1. Brazil – Politics and Government. 2. Economic History. 3. Inflation. 4. Militarism. 5. Economic Politics. I. Title

DDC 338.981

RAVENNA EFFECT - THE COUP D'ÉTAT WAS CIVIL

ABSTRACT

This book seeks to clarify, first of all, the process of the 1964 coup d'état in Brazil, which was improperly characterized as a military coup, that was released on March 31. Such a reading of history was convenient for the generals while they held the top administration of the country, but it has been weighing against them since 1985, when the barracks intervention ended.

In order to give consistency to the arguments, the book unmasks the lies that are told about the issue and smashes the precedents of the civil coup, of the PSD, circumscribing them to the disorders caused by the Ravenna Effect, the installing of the chief os State residence in a city without a historical secular status of national capital.

Also in the book it is an analysis of the weaknesses and strengths of the vast country called Brazil.

RAVENNA EFFECT - THE COUP D'ÉTAT WAS CIVIL

Cacildo Marques

ÍNDICE

	Preface	x
	Prefácio to the second edition	xiii
1	On interests	1
2	On lies	6
3	On capitals	17
4	On adventures	27
5	On politics	49
6	On structures	72

PREFACE

Among the recommendation of Kant, that our judgement be always universal, and the one of Tolstoy, that who wants to be universal sings his village, I tried to stay in the middle of both.

Those who cloistered, poisoned and mutilated me in the dictatorship, with the objective of doing me to remain silent, now are dead. The time and the worms took charge of their task. Even with a foot behind, I speak, finally.

I wrote this work for the reader, who has it in his hands, and also to retake an old debate with university friends, among which the current Minister of the Civil House and the current President of the City Hall of Sao Paulo. I treat here of the Lusophone portion of South America. As we were almost one century under monarchic regime, we have specific psychological characteristics in the American continent. But as, before this, we almost passed one century under Spanish domain, we have more identity with the brothers of Hispanic speech of what we consider, while we continued to use the proclitic in the colloquial language and the Castilian form of the gerund, besides understanding what they speak, notwithstanding the contrary effort of television.

I didn't write this book to the pro-fascist conservatism, nor to the pro-conservative left, those two currents that embrace each other against the freedom and the social progress when the winds are favorable to them. If they intend to speak badly of this work, they will be provoking rain in the wet. Between those two types, we can identify the classic liberals, even the ones who imagine conservatives, and the progressives, from where I wait constructive critics come.

I inform at once that he who classifies me as pessimist with base in the analysis I present in these pages will be wrong. I see our possibilities starting from the search of the Peter's perspective, that "a thousand days are how one day", and of the relative faith in the 'Fifth Empire' delineated by Antonio Vieira. South America can come to be great in human development, if it changes the arrogance for the firm purpose of riding of the old skin that arrests it in a prejudicing world done of political illusions, economical losses and intellectual limitation.

Breaking the metal chains doesn't just mean to get rid of the physical jails. Freeing of the mental cave is more important and more urgent. Without this movement, we would be still today burning witches in the bonfire, for delirium of the masses, while judging to be this a correct and advanced attitude.

So that the historical times close its cycle we needed to give the necessary steps for making the human society to overcome the phase of embryo. And we won't make this if we don't have clear that the society, far away from being a fallen gift of heaven, is fruit of a risky engineering, which, if continues neglecting scale, square, level and plumb line, will destroy the world.

Cacildo Marques, April 2014.

Preface to the Second Edition in Portuguese

A small slip of the first edition, 2014, in the item "Proportional", on the election of Hitler as a representative in 1932, brought me the need to prepare this second edition of the book Ravenna Effect. There I had written that the election had taken place in the old district system, when, in fact, as I was able to ascertain later, the Weimar Constitution had instituted the proportional model, following Belgium, but in a timid manner, with a profusion of competing parties and a large number of electoral districts (35), which compromised the health of the new method. Such a scarecrow led the Germans to develop trauma of the proportional method, with the introduction, post-Nazism, of the so-called mixed district vote.

Verifying my own failure (I did not receive readers' warning), I decided to delve into the differences between the district and proportional systems. I have read the 1870 French first edition of Jules Borely's "Nouveau Sistème Électoral", and then I translated to both English and Portuguese, since there was not yet a version for either language. The reason for the delay in the translation, at least in the Portuguese-speaking case, was the publication in 1875, in Paris, in Spanish language, of the work "La Democracia Práctica", by Uruguayan-Argentinean judge Luis Vicente Varela, who said to make corrections to the Borely's book. Varela, unfortunately, rejected, for not understanding them, some crucial points of the proposal. The most serious one was not respecting the insistence on the vote in political party, which would form the proportion of seats in Parliament. Borely calls this "double simultaneous vote", which charges the voter the vote first in the party, then in the name of the candidate. Varela countered this by arguing that the voter is not clear enough to vote in a party program, and therefore should vote for names. Now, in Borely's proposal, the voter must be politically instructed to vote in a party. The vote there has to be compulsory for all those over 21 years old and the system has to literate every citizen. As for the number of competing parties, Borely's book proposes three situations: three parties, five parties and seven parties, nothing more. A proportional election in which 28 parties obtain seats, as it was that of Germany in 1932, constitutes a perversion of democracy. All of Borely's effort was to avoid the classic bipartisanship of the district vote, but allowing dozens of parties in the elections foretells tragedy or roguishness.

My translations are published with the titles of "Voto Proporcional", in Portuguese, and "Proportional Representation", in English.

Some other minor flaws were corrected to this second edition, without the pretension of exhausting the possibilities of improvement of the work.

The book argues that the 1964 coup was civil, but it is important to emphasize now, in 2018, that it would not be seen as a coup if the power, taken from the hands of Joao Goulart, had not been delivered to military forces two weeks later, by an injunction of Carlos Lacerda.

Another point that needs mention here is the list of the ten Brazilian defects, in the item "Defects". As the reader can verify, each of those defects bears the name of an author, responsible for identifying the problem. My contribution was to group them together. However, after the first edition to come to light, I noticed two defects, which, I claim, are my findings. The first was already mentioned in the Preface, without my realizing it was one of them, for it was not easy to assimilate the idea. I am speaking on "arrogance". We Brazilians are subtly arrogant, without realizing it. For example, we speak lousily on the country at any opportunity, but we do not allow foreigners to do so. We want the foreigner to swallow what we think he has to think is best, regardless of his will. For example, we sent to compete for the Oscar the film that we want to impose as the best, not the one that in the eyes of the foreigner would be the best indeed. The subtle "arrogance" is our 11th defect.

Our 12th defect is even more difficult to admit: the "carpet pull". We are always working so our compatriot does not do well. If in a musical festival the best composer of the country appears, the jurors give him the second place, at most. It is something like the

"Schadenfreude" of the Germans, the jubilation for the failure of the fellow, but it is more serious, because it involves an action to overthrow the other.

Of course, the book also contains the ten qualities, or virtues, of Brazilians.

Anyway, saying all these things in a preface may scare the reader, but at some point I would have to stop keeping them for myself. Without diagnosis, pathologies tend to expand, not cure.

Cacildo Marques, March 2018.

RAVENNA EFFECT - THE COUP D'ÉTAT WAS CIVIL

Cacildo Marques

1. On interests

Impossibility. Why cannot the interests in Brazil be reduced to civilized levels?

We will begin for this almost mystery that bestirs all the thinking beings.

Before 1994 this was not a relevant subject, because everybody understood that in regime of high inflation there was not how living together with low interests. But since the plan of stabilization applied by President Itamar Franco brought the inflation taxes to bearable levels, the attempts of doing the interest and the exchange to be held with civility have been bringing insomnia to the persons responsible for the economical politics.

It happens that high inflation, super evaluated exchange and interests above the reasonable are the three symptoms of a sick currency. The Real Plan did not intend to cure the Brazilian macroeconomics, but just to tame the manifestation of the inflationary pulse. From a book that presented the paths to solve the problem, the technicians of the Treasury used a single page when of the elaboration of the plan of stabilization.

Losing. Who loses with the inflation?

The inflation reaches big and small ones, with smaller damages among those who know manipulate the finance market. For the ones who are not rentist, the loss is the largest that one can imagine. For a monthly inflation of 100%, a worker who had kept under the mattress a note of 5 m. u. (five monetary units), enough to buy a kilo of tomato, he would see after 30 days that his money could buy only half kilo of the product, because the kilo of tomato no longer would cost 5 m. u., but 10 m. u. The result is that the worker has lost half of the value that he had kept.

If the fantasy of the 'inflationary tribute' worked, the government would not have a lot of motivation to suffocate the effect of the inflation, because it would be winning. But the government does not win with that, although the banks, which are the main rentist, and other players of the finances, know how to guard against that and to maintain their values, while most loses. With this, by a type of domestic exchange arbitration, some persons are going being richer and other more poor, in inflationary regime. As the loss is for most, the governments are urged to find a solution for the problem.

Guilty. Who carries the blame for the existence of high inflation?

Still more serious, the voters are a solid sure that every inflationary process arises under responsibility of the government, which ultimately is who manufactures the money. If next month the printed money has half of the value that it has today, in the common citizen's mind this is work of the government, and of anybody more. The voter gets right when he sees in the ruler the responsible for the loss, but he wanders when imagines that the government has clarity of what is doing. If it was something so simple, as it seems to be in the books written by the memorable and nice monetarist Milton Friedman, no government would live together with an inflation regime, because the public's rage is not something pleasant of facing. For Milton Friedman, inflation only exists by impression of money, then, it is enough the government to stop printing. This is very easy, but useless, because based on a fallacy.

So, it was of the Brazilian government's concerning in 1994 to stabilize the value of the currency, by the control of the inflation. Interests and exchange rate would be problems to be treated later.

Limit. Is a matter of legislation the adoption of a maximum limit of interest rate?

The representatives of 1988 had approved an article in the Federal Constitution limiting to 12% per year the basic tax of interests of the country, with base in the low interests practiced in the year of 1986, during the validity of the ephemeral Cruzado Plan. The problem is that, after the promulgation of the Constitution, nothing that one made was able to give an account of bringing the interests' rate for that level.

President Fernando Henrique Cardoso, FHC, had gotten, thanks to the calm that the plan of stabilization had propitiated, to abolish the precept of the prohibition to the presidential reelection, which was in force from the fall of the New State, in 1945. Then, while getting to reelect to the presidency, he had close to the end of his period the purpose of lowering the interests, because the service of the debt was exhausting the country. The president of the Central Bank, Arminio Fraga, surrendered to this task, and gradually the Copom (Council of Monetary Politics) was reducing the taxes, for happiness of Brazilians. When that fall arrived to the height of the 14,5%, the inflation arose again. Of course the reduction arrived to a reckless level. Then Fraga retook the discharge path, so that on the eve of the presidential election, which could not more be run by FHC, who was already in his second term (his project was of copying the system of the USA, which lowered of infinite reelections for just one, while in Brazil the number of reelections arose of zero to one), the taxes were in level very high, above the 22% per year. This facilitated in 2002 the victory of the Party of the Workers, still more because the candidate to the vice-presidency in the platform, entrepreneur Jose Alencar, had as life objective the reduction of the interest rates.

Among the several dozens of reforms suffered by the Constitution, it is counted the article that limited the interest rates, because, besides creating the consensus that this was not a constitutional matter, the politicians began to conform to the fatality of living under a regime of high interest.

Banks. Why are the market interests much higher than the basic tax?

After ten years, the technicians forgot the experience of Arminio Fraga. Or, more probably, they thought Fraga didn't know how to apply the reduction plan, and that in 2012 the new technicians of the Central Bank were already endowed with that science. And one began a project of slow reduction. Before this, one has created the myth that the inflation was thing of the past, and that the country was already free from new strikes. Even respectable economists hammered this new superstition. And it came being reinforced by the fact that the reduction of the interests had arrived to a much lower level than that of the FHC government: the Selic (Special System of Clearance Sale and Custody) rate of the Central Bank went down to the number of 7,25%. As they didn't see the explanation for this difference, they began to believe that there was no more inflationary risk. And the explanation was very simple: with the extinction of the state public banks since the end of the FHC government, the level of the 'spread', the value of the market interest rate, was maintained in the heights by the private banks, against which the Federal Economic Cashier and the Bank of Brazil (Banco do Brasil) could do almost nothing. Only when President Dilma Rousseff has begun strong pressure on those banks, in the beginning of 2013, it was that the market rates started to lower, in sense contrary to the inflation index. Certainly, much better for the government would have been to leave the banks to collect their rates of 180% per year, what was not good for the consumers of appliances, but that was constituted in a mechanism of defense of the economy, holding the inflation. With the Selic rate low, the government would pay very reduced interests in the service of the debt and, for administrative effect, although not electoral, that would be very positive.

Repetition. Was very reckless to reduce the interests a lot in 2012?

Who knows the operation of the Brazilian macroeconomics knew the future result of that politics of pressing for the fall of interests. One just waited the day in that the youth, as in the Collor government, in 1992, when the plans of control of the inflation failed, would run to the streets in uncontrolled crowds demanding changes.

That happened in 2013 June, when the governments of the State and of the city of Sao Paulo announced the new increase in the price of the tickets of urban buses, metropolitan trains and subway, increase that came being postponed from the beginning of that year, exactly in order to weigh less in the inflation. For the buses, the increase was of twenty cents, and the activists incorporated among their order words this that "it is not only for the twenty cents", while leaving explicit that the revolt felt for several other reasons, including the price of the kilo of the tomato, which arose from 2 m. u. to 18 m. u. in a matter of a few weeks.

But we pass now to the subjects of politics, education, health, industry, culture, religion, ethnicism, legislation, safety, habitation, energy, environment, tributes, job, income, geography and communications, among others. We will return to the macroeconomics in the final pages of this work.

2. On lies

Shock. Are all of the citizens open to the new ideas?

There are people who are angry simply by hearing or reading statements to contradict their faiths nurtured for a long time. This is the most expressive display of lack of resilience. The normal person disagrees, and is surprised when coming across with ideas that shock with his old convictions, but he makes this inside a mental process, without screams, grimaces or other physical manifestation, and soon he is recomposed, while absorbing the new data and putting it in the scale to decide if he substitutes his previous thought by the new one or if has good reason to maintain his old position.

This present work would not have been written if it was to compile current evaluations, which circulate as the most absolute truths. It is here to increase, no matter how much it can bewilder comfortable 'opinions'.

Kubitschek. Which historical episode did lead off the articulation of the coup of 1964?

We treated here then of the coup of April 1, 1964, shot off upon the presidency of the Republic by the Brazilian parliament. The egg of that tyrannosaurus was not released on August 24, 1954, with the suicide of Vargas, as someone already said, but on October 3, 1955, with the election to the presidency of the lieutenant-colonel policeman doctor Juscelino Kubitschek de Oliveira (PSD: Social Democratic Party). Juarez Tavora (UDN: National Democratic Union) and Adhemar de Barros (PSP: Progressive Social Party) had together 56% (30% and 26%) of the votes, while Kubitschek, the elect, got 36%. Plinio Salgado (PRP: Paulist Republican Party), fourth and last presidential candidate, obtained 8%. According to the Constitution of 1946, the vice president was chosen separately, and the election occurred in a unique round, because still the model of the second round, cathartic sophistication of the demagogy, copied of the Fifth Republic of France, had not been introduced in

Brazil. In the winner coalition, the vice was Joao Goulart (PTB: Brazilian Labor Party), nicknamed Jango, former minister of the Work. Kubitschek lost for Adhemar de Barros in SP, PR, AM and RO (then territory of Guapore), and lost for Tavora in five States of the Northeast (SE, AL, PE, PB and CE). One can see that the electoral backrest of Kubitschek was very fragile.

Jacareacanga. Was the Kubitschek government well accepted in its beginning?

When having taken the oath of office on January 31, 1956, Kubitschek had to face an attempt of military coup, initiated on February 10, when some officers of the Aeronautics deviated airplanes in the Field of Afonsos, Rio de Janeiro, for the air base of Jacareacanga, in Para', and dominated some close cities. Only after 19 days, the rebellion, known as 'Riot of Jacareacanga', was put down. Those soldiers accused the president of having strong connection with leftists and, therefore, intending to lead the country for the route of the socialism.

On November 11, just after the election, a coup well succeeded in the contrary sense had happened, and this perhaps has urged the military of the Aeronautics in their action. Marshal Henrique Teixeira Lott deposed the interim president, Carlos Luz, because there were strong noises that he worked to impede the oath of Kubitschek. In his place, the president of the Senate, Nereu Ramos, was raised to the interim presidency of the country. Lott had high pretensions, because five years later he ran to the presidency, by the coalition PSD-PTB, when he lost for Janio Quadros (PTN: National Labor Party).

Works. Which good work did Kubitschek leave as a legacy?

When one asks to some Brazilian which are the important works of the Kubitschek government, soon the changing of the capital for Brasilia and the installation of new automotive industries by German and North American companies come to mind. However, the enlargement of the industry of cars brought the shut down of the railways and the construction of Brasilia imposed to South America the tragedy of living under the Versailles-Weimar Effect decades after decades. The Plan of

Goals of Kubitschek was prepared by economist Roberto de Oliveira Campos, who never forgave the president for having fit in the project the pendant Brasilia. As Celso Furtado told, it was in a campaign assembly in Jatai (MG) that a man screamed to the candidate: "If you are said so good, why don't you build Brasilia?" Kubitschek decided on that moment the matter and answered: "Of course! I will build Brasilia!" One didn't improve soon afterwards if that challenging voter was or not a great proprietor of lands in the area of the savanna. Clear he was not certainly.

The UDN, opposition party to Vargas and Kubitschek, promoted long campaign against the construction of Brasilia. But, for unhappiness of the country, the party made that moved just by the opposition spirit, without knowing against what it was struggling, therefore the argument was just this of the public expenses. Now, that corresponded to the cost of a mere brick of the Palace of Versailles, given the misfortunes that the country would have to live the following decades. Ironically, Kubitschek was nicknamed 'President Bossa Nova', since the bossa nova was the great musical innovation that the world has just invented, what occurred in some carioca apartments, after a small period of self-confinement of guitarist Joao Gilberto in the city of Diamantina (MG), accidentally, the home town of Kubitschek. Far away of being president bossa nova, the President buried this musical gender, in the cemetery of the vicissitudes to which he submitted all of the Brazilians.

Unlike the UDN thought, the expenses of the construction of Brasilia would not have brought any problem to the country if the mission of the city had been other, different of that of sheltering the chief of State, as the one of being an industrial pole, the capital of a future State of Tocantins - or of the State of Planalto -, the headquarters of a great aeronautics school or a mystic-tourist center. With any other objective, the costs would have been paid quickly and the country would have achieved great earnings.

For reminding to those forgotten ones, the great work of Kubitschek, which only brought benefits, was the Dam of Oros, in

Ceara'.

Inflation. How did occur the beginning of the super inflation period?

Deputy Ulysses Guimaraes said, in one of his interviews to TV Cultura (SP), that Kubitschek called him to palace to expose him a great doubt. Would he owe or not to print money? If he printed, there would be the great risk of creating an inflationary period. If he didn't print, it would be for him difficult to tolerate the pressure of the unions for salary increases, because the population needed to do front to the shortage that propagated for the country. The known facts were the shortage and the pressure of the unions, not the super inflation, which still didn't pass of abstraction in the mind of Brazilians. Then Mr. Ulysses recommended: "President, rotate the guitar". The money became printed, the wages were increased and the prices received new increments. With new money impression and new increases of prices, the wild race among prices and banknotes began in that moment, for lasting almost forty years.

In 1958, coins issued in the Second Reign still circulated, showing the face of Don Pedro II. They had, obviously, small value, but had value still. Starting from the entrance of the inflation, those coins left circulation, some of them going to the museum, other for the garbage.

And like was already said, in 1994 a plan of stabilization was made with views to suffocate the inflationary pressures, which, as even the most naive economists know now, didn't cure the currency.

Militarism. What was the doctrinaire base of the formation of the military men?

In this 21st century we see that it is passed already the hour of a pact in the United Nations against the installation of military regimes, which had their role in the history in time in that the war was the language of the relationships among countries, whenever there was reason of tension. Early, a military one is trained to obey, and to make war, in defense of the homeland. In the top of the command, as a general, he has as ethos of work never to let someone to disobey him. A general who occupies the position of chief of State doesn't get to disentangle himself of this professional apprenticeship. It was like this that Napoleon Bonaparte, for instance, as president and as emperor, never stopped acting as military boss.

Under that rigorous training for the hierarchical obedience, a military man is rebelled by having to beat continence to another military who is of lower patent and for some reason has jumped over the position of supreme chief of his country. Corporal Adolf Hitler, lieutenant-colonel Juscelino Kubitschek and colonel Hugo Chavez had to face their subordinates' resistance in the barracks. It is a reckless choice this of abandoning the barracks without reaching the maximum patent, be in the police, be in the aeronautics, in the navy or in the army, and to look for cutting road while reaching the chair of chief of State, for putting under his command his old commanders. If to give office to a general as president can be the sign of a nightmare, to vest official of inferior patent is right nightmare.

Coup. Is there in Brazil a history of military governments coming via the military coups?

The Brazilian military men, since the beginning of the Republic, have some species of conscience in relation to the negative aura of military governments resulting of coups. Marshal Lott struck a coup, yes, in 1955, but to vest an elected man. In October 1930, military men gave a coup d'état, but after ten days they called lawyer Getulio Vargas to occupy the presidency of the Republic, and he has taken the oath on November 3.

And in 1964 the exactly contrary of the coup of 1930 happened: civilians gave a coup, on April 1, and after ten days called Marshal Castello Branco, who was confirmed in the presidency of the Republic by the National Congress on the April 11 and vested on the 15.

In that moment the lie of the century was built in South America.

It is strange that no old general has come to public attention to admit this fiction. The holders of the power have immense capacity to forge and to impose a speech. But there is one moment in which the things should be cleared up. A lot of people think that is irrelevant, but it is not so. The cessation of the maintenance of the farce will do well to the armed forces and to the way itself like they are seen by Brazilians.

There is who tries to argue in favor of the militarist version of the coup, while alleging that the generals were participant of the scheme. Now, never a coup purely civil has existed in any country, because the power is sustained by the armed forces and, if somebody undertakes the deposition of a chief of State, some military support he has for back, or he will be seen soon afterwards as a jester or as a demented. Then what distinguishes a civil coup of a military coup is the nature of the leadership of the action. If a military man is who puts the tip of the bayonet in the ruler's throat and throws him down, the coup is soldierly. If a civilian is who signs the deposition action, or who gives an oral ultimatum, not matter how many legions defend it, this is a civil coup d'état. Otherwise, civilians would be always the good young men of the history, because they would never have as applying a coup. And who wants examples of military governing after soldiers to apply coup d'état doesn't need to go very far: it is enough to study the cases on Augusto Pinochet Ugarte, in Chile (1973), and Jorge Rafael Videla, in Argentina (1976).

Revolution. Where we can find sources telling about 'civil coup' in 1964?

There is a special number of the magazine O Cruzeiro, in Portuguese, on the coup of April 1. The edition came out on April 10 (see in http://bit.ly/2Fz96l2), when commemorating the 'civil revolution'. The editors didn't suspect that already on the April 9 the delivery of the government to the generals had been in agreement, and that on the 11 the National Congress would choose Marshal Humberto de Alencar Castello Branco as president of Brazil. Any other reports of the great press published on those first ten days of April 1964 will bring the same chronicle of civil coup, although they don't use the word 'coup'.

All of the people know what happened from then, but they

continue buying the version built by the military government.

The coup of April 1 was unfurled by the president of the Senate, Auro Soares de Moura Andrade (PSD-SP), aided by the revolt of the population against the inflation and by the governors of Sao Paulo, Guanabara (Rio city), Minas, Bahia and others.

When decreed the deposition of Jango, in the first hour of the dawn, the activists certified that the bosses of the Army, explicit defenders of the 'legality', would not be revolted against that action. The day was very tense. While the activist governors brought for their side the commanders that were close, the III Army's commander, of Rio Grande do Sul, only came to adhere to the movement at the 20 hours of that April 1. Then before of that schedule nobody knew if the chief of State was really Ranieri Mazzilli or would be Joao Goulart again, or a confrontation there would be been among the troops loyal to the deposed president and those loyal to the insurgents. As the Gaucho officials are not crazy, after a complete day of evaluations, they gave up, for sadness of Leonel Brizola, who waited more lingering resistance.

Re-writing. How was the farce built?

From that the hilarious creation of the coup's description came. There are usually displacements of troops inside the country, because this is part of the military routine. On the eve of the April 1, the Army knew that General Mourao Filho had brought his battalion from Juiz de Fora toward the Fluminensis North, where he has been with other military bosses and where they fraternized. It consists that the objective of General Mourao was to lead his military detachment to the city of Rio de Janeiro, because, maybe, he had not been informed that the capital of the country had been moved to Brasilia, on the opposite side, four years before, nor that the city, which was the State of Guanabara, came being already governed by the conservatives, in the person of Carlos Lacerda. Even so, the action was the great discovery of the military men! The General Mourao's displacement was ordained, later, as the great military action that engendered the coup, which was called after 'Redeemer Revolution'. Certainly, neither Darcy Ribeiro, Minister-chief of the Civil

House, nor the presidency of the Congress knew about this. They have come to know together with all of the Brazilians, some days later, when Castello Branco was vested and his assistants were manufacturing the historiography. It was without knowing of General Mourao that Darcy Ribeiro, in the first minutes of the April 1, when taking knowledge of the proposal for the president deposition, ordered message to the Senate: "If they depose Jango, I can order the military device to close the National Congress". Senator Moura Andrade, who minutes before had despised Darcy Ribeiro message about the trip of Joao Goulart to Porto Alegre, picked a fight and made to approve the deposition of the president of the country, and the military device remained silent, perplexed. How could they to face the PSD?

No chief of State is safe on his chair when the inflation corrodes the government. Neither Romulus Augustulus (476), nor Louis XVI (1793), nor Abraham Lincoln (1865), nor Franz Joseph I (1914), nor Friedrich Ebert (1919), none of those was safe while the discharge of prices tormented his population.

Prizes. What relevance did have General Mourao in the military governments?

Mourao received as prize for yours 'precedence' in those events just an evanescent temporary presidency of military tribunal, because he entered the history as Pilate entered the credo, by triangulation. And he was later severely criticized by Governor Magalhaes Pinto, for having set up his supposed 'skirmish' of the March 31.

The main activists of the coup were: Auro Soares de Moura Andrade (SP), Magalhaes Pinto (MG), Adhemar de Barros (SP), Carlos Lacerda (GB), Assis Chateaubriand (SP), Julio de Mesquita Filho (SP) and Roberto Marinho (GB).

And why did the civil activists give the government to the generals? It is very easy to understand this. Ranieri Mazzilli didn't have enough leadership to solve the economical problems that generated the coup. The prices would continue to arise and the interim president would be dropped of a way or other. Before he was dropped by the left-wing, regimented by the trade-unionist leaderships and leaning by some military allied to Brizola, Magalhaes Pinto (called by the magazine O Cruzeiro 'the Hero of the Revolution' and leaning for the ambassador of the United States and his Democratic Party, which was in the American government), Moura Andrade and others opted to call the armed forces.

It would be not well for the generals to order to register in the books of history that they won the government as a present of a coward right wing. Then the events were retroactive in 11 days, they super dimensioned General Mourao's exercise and fastened, authoritatively, the date of the fictitious coup on March 31.

Fiasco. Were the military men better for having not been authors of the coup?

Entering the decision of the coup d'état as subsidiary doesn't make the military men better. They would only have been better if they had not accepted to head that government resulting of a coup they didn't forge, since they were defensive of the 'legality'. Did they have previous plans to Brazil? They always had, obviously. And why didn't they reveal later the factual truth of those days, while apologizing? Because the nonsense they made and the role they exercised in the sequence were so catastrophic that they have evaluated to be better to maintain silence. Besides, so much the skeptics Castello, Orlando Geisel, Ernesto Geisel and Golbery, as the dogmatic Costa e Silva, Medici, Sylvio Frota, Figueiredo, Meira Mattos and Rademaker, the great bosses who slipped, in the two lines, all of them are died.

The civil entrepreneurs who were allied of the dictatorship bear testimonies, are justified and reply, but they don't help to explain the facts, because they are considered supporting, or backers. Now, it is not this what makes the coup a 'civil-military' coup. The unquestionable fact is that the coup was fired by conservative civilians. The military men entered later to accomplish their orders, as armed partners. Obviously, some of those, like Carlos Lacerda, didn't understand the game and were banished, because little by little the generals went noticing that, if the supreme leadership of the country was given them, they would not have to obey to politicians' orders, not even of those that gave them oath. On the contrary, the order of the day starting from there came to be the withholding, the banishment and other forms of persecution of the rebels who refused to accept their orders.

Correction. Is it very expensive to undo the already consolidated lies?

Lies are wrought the whole time, and Brazil not even is the more prodigal in this art. What one should have in account always is that the harmful lies need to be undone. Recently a great statistical manipulation was winning the credulous people's minds, and this was the myth of the full employment, built starting from defective methods of the IBGE, the Institute of Geography and Statistics. Traditionally, it is considered that the level of full employment is reached when 1% of unemployed are had in the market, what happened in 1944 in the United States. In Brazil, for the rudimentary calculation that they were publishing, the tax was between 4% and 5%. Even so, the credulous ones hammered that the country lived the abundance of the full employment, against all of the empirical evidences. Finally, on January 16, 2014, the IBGE announced that it had a new statistic, built on new bases. Before, six metropolitan areas were researched. In the new method, all of the metropolitan areas of the country are covered. On the pretext of introducing the new method, the unjustified lie was abandoned. The rate of official unemployment of Brazil became 7,4%.

Respect. Will the Brazilian military men always be suspects of scheming coup d'état?

It doesn't suit to the Brazilian military men today to carry in the backs this stain that associates them to activists and disrespecting of the laws and institutions. Under the influence of that badly told history, conservative youths, in several corners of the country, shout for military intervention against governments that they didn't choose, since they have voted for defeated candidate. The military men have their political convictions, but they undergo their constitutional role. If fascist youths ask for a quartered, they need to receive as answer the information that the Brazilian military men receive solid formation to do to be worth the dictates of the law. And so that this answer has sense, the youths need to know that military governments of the Brazilian past didn't happen via the coups fired by generals. This means that the military ones themselves need to give up the fiction of April, which they adopted as having been factual history.

3. On capitals

Decades. Are there available writings on the role of the national capitals in the history?

This author already treated the subject of this chapter in other books published previously, but he didn't notice sign that he had been understood until today, for this the inclusion here is done. The first book was "*Brasilia - capital of the fair weather?*" of 1988, how development of a small text written in 1975. Soon afterwards, "*Ten ways to abolish the inflation*", of 1993. In 1997, "*How to build a world only of wealth*" and, finally, in 2012, "*The Brussels Crisis*".

It is a study developed along many years, while incorporating, of times in times, new unquestionable facts, which, as one can see by the dates above, have ripening period going from 1975 to 2012, in an extension, therefore, of 37 years, at least.

During the work of the writing of '*The Brussels Crisis*', in the 31 days of January of 2012, the author found a link until then lost, which was the perception that the First World War was also submitted to the umbrella of this concept greatly analyzed, which receives the name of Versailles-Weimar Effect, or Ravenna Effect.

Versailles. Which is the core of the concept of Versailles-Weimar Effect?

For explaining the concept of the Versailles-Weimar Effect would be possible to write a book of thousands of pages, but it can also be summarized in half page, or little more. In this present work, he will come in a way very summarized, even because, as it was said above, it has already been developed in previous books.

The name Ravenna Effect, or Versailles-Weimar Effect, which was just Versailles Effect in the beginning, changed because other studious had already used this more simplified form to represent another phenomenon (which was this of the export of habits and fashions), was born of the comparison of the economical and social consequences of the adoption of the capital Brasilia with the one of the capital Versailles, both seen as new cities, in their time. The original sketch of the concept broke of the idea that upsets in the life of society are inevitable when the supreme power of a country is installed in recently built city. More ahead, the name 'Weimar' was added to the concept because the vision was enlarged. The upset doesn't just happen under the influx of a new city, but of any capital without secular status of residence of the major leader. Also the name Weimar Effect was already used for other studious to designate the impoverishment of the population under the action of the hyperinflation, defined for Phillip Cagan as the inflation regime with taxes larger than 50% per month.

So, a country is ridden of the Versailles-Weimar Effect, or Ravenna Effect, if, first, it doesn't suffer a stronger neighbor's political-geographical influence, not necessarily contiguous, which is living that problem - Portugal in relation to France in 1789, for instance - and, second, it has its hegemonic capital installed by at least 120 years in the same city, which acquired, then, secular status of capital. Examples are Japan today, but not the one of 1869, with Mutsuhito recently installed in Tokyo, China today, but not the one of 1949, with President Chiang Kai-Shek installed in Nanjing, and Yank America today, but not the one of 1861, during the Secession War, under influence of a capital Washington still without secular status.

Concept. How does the Versailles-Weimar Effect work after all?

Before mentioning cases of countries that are under the effect in this millennium beginning, it is convenient to do a summary of the theory.

The break of the bonds with the leaders of society, in the search for a new elite, what is characterized by the change of the chief of State for another city that is not the one that holds the status of secular capital, inaugurates in the mind of the citizens a psychosocial state contemptuous to the consolidated symbols. Practically all of the patriotic symbols, accompanying the abandoned capital, suffer that wastage, but what provokes larger damage is the depreciation of the money. Mechanisms can be developed and implanted with aim to suffocate the inflation, but not the inflationary pulse. This only disappears with the cessation of the new presidential residence, or with the substitution of the status, after 120 years, as it happened with the new capitals Tokyo and Washington. Although technicians find ways to control inflation, interest and exchange, the problem of the liquidity and credit remains, because the dragon needs to breathe. It is pure insanity to want to outline the situation with measures of neopalacian sustaining. This was justifiable in the 18th century, when rulers and ministers were innocent in relation to the monetary and financial knowledge.

Those courtiers who manage society, who are changed automatically when the chief of State abandons them and goes to a new capital, don't form a small group of people: they are the city. And even if a crazy tyrant decided to change the capital taking all of the inhabitants of the old capital for the new, these would not be in their habitat, but, yes, moved in a new atmosphere, as any upstarts. The substitution of the social hegemonic class of the country is inevitable when one settles a recent capital.

And this is the reason because the effect was not noticed along the history, at least up to 1975: the longevity of its action, which escapes to the usual paradigms. Maybe one doesn't come to discover any other phenomenon of social change whose effect lasts more than a hundred years.

Application. Has the concept been verified in practice?

When a psychosocial pattern is discovered, the way of confirming it is to apply it to the historical facts. And when it is something that brings high costs it is more comfortable to do this with situations of the past. The first confirmation has occurred through a bet, without money involved, obviously. In a lecture in the Ibero-Americana College (Unibero), in Sao Paulo, the author affirmed that in the year 476, year of the fall of the Roman Empire of the Occident, certainly the imperial residence was not installed in Rome. How is this? Where was it? The students asked, but the author didn't know, because the courses of History were never concerned with the social role of capitals. There was not Internet still. The author would research and he would send the answer in another day. Returning home, a fast consultation to manuals brought the answer: Ravenna. Emperor Honorius had changed the imperial residence for that city in 402. When in 476 Romulus Augustulus was knocked down, while losing the empire for the barbaric invaders, he lived in Ravenna, not in Rome. Something that one can imagine is that the invaders were well received in the abandoned capital, Rome. Fact. What happened was really this, whereas the Romans no longer tolerated so many civil wars, so many provincial rebellions and so much shortage.

In that same phase, the author consulted Professor Siang Wu Sun, of computation, in the USP (University of Sao Paulo). In what city was Chiang Kai-Shek when the Mao Tse-Tung's revolutionaries entered Peking and took the power in 1949? Lightning-answer of Professor Sun: Nanjing.

Vienna. Except Versailles and Weimar, there is any case really notable to which is the idea applied?

The most recent verification didn't involve third persons. It was the case of the First World War. Such great events in the modern history involve always increasing of prices. The manuals say that archduke Franz Ferdinand, heir of the Austro-Hungarian throne, was murdered by an activist in the streets of Sarajevo and this unchained the war. The impression that the books leave in the students' mind is that the activist, crazy or not, had some personal antipathy for the future monarch and killed him. An anarchist? Maybe. But it is not common anarchists to go shooting futures chiefs of State, just because they don't want to live under constituted governments. The thing was more reasonable (not that any crimes can be justified): the Austro-Hungarian currency was sick. The inflation rates grew in that distant 1914. But the capital was not in Vienna? Almost!

Empress Elisabeth of Bavaria, the famous Sissi, came being seconded, for a long time, by actress Katharina Schratt, known as empress without crown, who was maintained by Emperor Franz Joseph I not in Vienna, but in Bad Ischl's city. And for the subjects, it doesn't matter where the emperor lives officially, but where he stays overnight systematically. The disaster was mounted.

Paris. How did the effect occur in France itself, which has inspired the discovery?

The case of Versailles has been base, not an object of confirmation. But to the ones who imagine that the French Revolution only broke out because of the preaching of some philosophers, and there is who believes in this still, it suits to ammunition them with data. It is known that in the morning of July 14, 1789, it didn't happen anything of very special before the crowd to take Bastille and to loosen the prisoners, but in the previous day, July 13, the important registered fact is that the government authorized, for ordinance, an increase of 100% in the price of the bread. Meanwhile, Louis XVI was in the Palace of Versailles, while seeing Marie Antoinette to take care of her goats and roses.

The city, obviously, should not be blamed of the political and economical disasters: the fault is in the people's decision. So, one should enroll that Louis XVI didn't build a scaffold for himself, but he inherited it indirectly. The transfer of the court for Versailles happened on May 6, 1682, under Louis XIV. Little more than one century later, Louis XVI was beheaded, not like a fool, as the columnists registered, but like a martyr, because he had accepted few days before the revolutionaries' demand for the rehabilitation of the real residence in the Palace of Louvre, at Paris. The fatidic century of Versailles was finished. Certainly, the indisposition that this created among the enemies of the abrupt changes, even if restorative, added to the wave of beheadings in the Square of the Concordance, took the panic to the interior of the palace, making him to gamble the frustrated and tragic attempt of escape for Varrenes. The real couple died without having enjoyed the glory of the decision to return to Louvre, while leaving this for Napoleon Bonaparte, because also Robespierre, author of the Law of the Maximum, the freeze of prices that would be constituted in the necessary juridical step to put down the inflation definitively, was beheaded equally little later.

It suits to remind that Louis XVI was not the only martyr for Paris. Three centuries before, Joan of Arc, in her eighteen years old and with a trace of successive victories against English ahead of the French troops, decided, even without the formal support that until that moment she came having of Charles VII, the dolphin whom she made to crown, to retake Paris for France. In that itinerary, she had to retake the cities that were in the hands of English and, even when having received the help of the Italian army of Berthelemy Baretta, in the battle for the rescue of the city of Compiègne she was captured finally by enemies, to die in the bonfire one year later, by a process polluted for frauds.

Goulart. Under this effect, would there be some possibility of Goulart to finish his mandate?

In Brazil, the beginning of the year of 1964 found President Joao Goulart curled with an inflation more and more growing, which came corroding the country since Kubitschek decided "to spin round the guitar", i. e., to print money to do front to the discharge of prices. While imitating his political godfather Getulio Vargas, Goulart also decreed increase of 100% in the minimum wage. Unlike the action of Vargas, in the beginning of the fifties, this increase now didn't help a lot, because it just covered last inflation and was ahead to new chiming that certainly would come. And they came, while doing the chief of State to start to govern as if he stepped on eggs. On March 31, 1964, he didn't take a flight to Rio de Janeiro, the capital abandoned some years before. He flew to Porto Alegre, to join his brother-in-law Leonel Brizola, former-governor of Rio Grande do Sul. The rumor that circulated among the conservatives in Brasilia was that he had left to Uruguay, without any formal communication. Then, instigated by the governors of most populous States, the Senate decreed his deposition, in the first hour of the dawn of April 1.

There was an established path with views to do Joao Goulart to complete the mandate that he inherited of Janio Quadros when this resigned in 1961: the parliamentarism. As well as in the weeks that preceded the oath of Kubitschek, the conservatives' resistance to accept the oath of Goulart was very big, so much in the civil middle as among the military ones. Then general Ernesto Geisel, boss of the Military House of the interim president Ranieri Mazzili in those agitated days that were succeeded to the presidential resignation, presented his suggestion for solving the impasse, which was the acceptance of the oath under the condition that the president implanted the parliamentarism. The agreement consolidated and Goulart took oath, while having Tancredo Neves as premier, but, for influence of Brizola, a provocative clause was introduced: in January 1963, it would be summoned a plebiscite so that the population said yes or not to the return of the presidentialism. After the short periods of Tancredo Neves and Hermes Lima in the government's leadership, Goulart, as way of showing that he was open to the conciliation, vested in the end of 1962 as premier Senator Auro Soares de Moura Andrade (PSD-SP), an ally, however conservative. This noticed that he would govern for a very small period, given that the chance of approval of the parliamentarism in the plebiscite was very low. Therefore he demanded the president postponed the plebiscite, without knowing that this was a dogmatic matter in the mind of Goulart and Brizola. The president didn't give in and the premier gave up the position, after having exercised it for only 24 hours, insufficient time to include his passage at the government in the books of History of the medium teaching. Goulart invited then for being premier Francisco de Paula Brochado da Rocha, an ally of him from Rio Grande do Sul, brought of the trade-unionist environment.

Deposition. Did Goulart then underestimate the destructive power of the inflation?

In January 1963, the population manifested about the return of the presidentialism. In the fifteen following months, Moura Andrade and his co-religionists were dedicated to the elaboration of the plan of the president's deposition, a plan helped for many imperial decisions that the president started to make, wrapped by the clout that he judged to have acquired with the victory in the plebiscite, as the Law of

Remittance of Profits (which rioted investors and government from the United States), the instruction 242 of Sumoc - Superintendence of the Currency and Credit (which threw the debt of import of capital goods of the private national companies in the backs of the Bank of Brazil, while transforming private debt in public debt) - and the break of the military hierarchy, in the fraternization done with the Club of the Sergeants without participation or approval of the generals.

A suicide person can drink poison and to die soon afterwards, by cardiac crash, or breathing stop. Who wants it, this one can believe since then that the "causa mortis" was the stop, be cardiac, be respiratory. But who accompanied the process and who did the autopsy in the Legal Medical Institute know that the death was provoked by the poison. In the same way, the ones who have full conviction that Joao Goulart was only dropped because of the cruelty of conservatives, have the right of continuing to have faith in this. The true cause, however, was the same that dropped the Roman Empire and the Austro-Hungarian Empire and drew of the power Louis XVI and Chiang Kai-Shek: inflation.

Who doesn't believe in this, with very less reason can believe that those and other countless cases of destruction happened because of change of capital, the Ravenna Effect. Nobody is forced to believe in what doesn't want, but he cannot since ever allege that the warning has not been given.

History. Is it difficult to do a roll of the tragedies that had as base the effect?

From a lot before the introduction of the paper money in the economy, what happened in China on January 12, 1024, the shortage tormented the people, although the inflation was hindered by the small possibility of replacement of the money. But, unlike what some economists imply, the release of the paper money didn't bring inflation in the first decades. Only one century later, in 1127, the loss of value of the Chinese currency was registered for the first time. This was due to the change of the capital, from Kaifeng to Hangzhou, on that same year, when the Jin dynasty incorporated the Chinese north and forced the

Song dynasty to move for the South. It was, therefore, in function of military defeat, which dislodged the emperor of his residence, and not for some pharaonic impulse of construction of new capital, that the inflation of China corroded and damaged for several centuries its important invention, which was the paper money.

While taking as much the cases of devastating shortage as the one of inflation, the report of falls of empires or emperors forced by the Ravenna Effect includes at least the cases below.

    1353 BC - Reign of Akhenaten, in Aten (Amarna), which ruined Egypt.
    931 BC - Division, post-Solomon, of the kingdom whose capital David installed in Jerusalem.
    323 BC - Death of Alexander in his new capital Alexandria, and disassembling of the empire.
    476 - Fall of the Roman Empire, with the imperial residence in Ravenna since 402.
    1561 - Residence of Philip II in Madrid, in 1561, and "Revolution of Prices" in 1568.
    1800 - Construction of Washington-DC, set on fire in 1812, with secession in 1861.
    1682 - Installation of the French court in Versailles, which led to the Revolution in 1789.
    1869 - Transfer of the capital of Japan for Tokyo, while following by Diaspora and wars.
    1919 - Beginning of the Weimar Republic: it brought hyperinflation and led to the Nazism.
    1946 - Presidential refuge in the Balaton Lake, Hungary: larger inflation in the history.
    1949 - Presidency of China in Nanjing, while provoking hyperinflation and revolution.
    1994 - Itinerant capitals in Balkans, post-Tito, with hyperinflation and war of Bosnia.

Today. Who is experiencing on these days the Versailles-Weimar Effect?

The most recent case of Ravenna Effect is the European Union, which after becoming a monetary union decided to form a federation in fact, with a president's election. Now, the presidential residence of the European Union was installed in the administrative capital, Brussels, which is a capital with secondary status in Western Europe. The president would have to live in Paris, maybe Berlin, if the Europeans recognize more the German capital as their main capital among the member States (N.: Maybe Brussels achieves fast status of capital, since it was already national secular capital). Before this case, we had Abuja, 1991, in Nigeria, and Borrowdale Brook, 2006, in Zimbabwe. And among them the case of Naypyidaw, 2005, the new capital of Myanmar (former Burma), country that, like Brazil and Turkey, suffered a lingering military regime. The capital of Turkey, Ankara, works in the same city since 1923, and is almost about to consolidate.

For relief of the ones that defend the maintenance of the new capitals, the solution of the 'Enigma of Berlin' came in 1993. The reason for which the capital Bonn, which worked during the years of the Federal Republic of Germany, separated from the German Democratic Republic, didn't bring the upset of the inflation was deciphered. Bonn didn't have capital status, and, nevertheless, the Ravenna Effect was not verified in it. The explanation is: the new capital is only harmful when one settles in it the chief of State. The premier and all the remaining of the government can stay in it, without problem. In the German case, the President always stayed in Berlin, even with the wall that separated the oriental part of the western part, and that was dropped in 1989. Therefore, for the European Union, there is no need to remove the European Parliament or the Administrative Commission from the city of Brussels. It is enough to remove from there the residence of the president of the European Council.

To Nigeria, it is enough to install the president in Lagos. Zimbabwe, which gave up on having own currency, simply needs to return the presidency to his old palace, in Harare. Also the president of Myanmar only needs to return to the old capital, Rangoon. And, for Brazil, just to install the presidential residence in Rio de Janeiro, while maintaining all the remaining of the government in Brasilia, governed by the minister-chief of the Civil House.

4. On advantages

Virtues. Are there Brazilian virtues to identify as valuable social capital?

Everybody knows that Brazil never made to respect as country because it lacks something subtle, which needs to be explained, not because it doesn't have high potentialities.

The advantages of the country are countless, and many of them are seen by Brazilians as wrong thing, thing that brings shame, just because it doesn't reproduce the rituals or the drawings of the model, which before it was France and today it is the United States. Few persons notice that the United States are much superiors in technology, and, therefore, in material wealth, but they are a lot behind Brazil in many aspects of the juridical-politics organization.

In the purely psychological extent, which comes from the history and from the culture of the country, it suits to reproduce what here was published already some years ago in the internet (it is enough to type at a search engine "Estigma de Pindorama"), which is the group of virtues common to the almost totality of the Brazilians, identified for unsuspicious intellectuals.

1. Courage (Ruy Barbosa);
2. Faith (Adelia Prado);
3. Patience (Alberto Moravia);
4. Sensibility (Darcy Ribeiro);
5. Generosity (Don Paulo Evaristo Arns);
6. Cordiality (Sergio Buarque de Holanda);
7. Happiness (Mario de Andrade);
8. Diligence (Roberto DaMatta);
9. Tolerance (Stefan Zweig);
10. Receptivity (Jose Bonifacio de Andrada e Silva).

Bonifacio still increases other ten behavioral aspects, while affirming that Brazilians are: (a) enthusiasts of the ideal; (b) friends of the freedom; (c) enemies of the arbitrariness; (d) talented, even when without instruction; (e) imaginative; (f) adherents of ennobling innovations; (g) generous; (h) capable of great actions, although not systematized; (i) impassioned by sex; (j) enterprising, although hardly conclude projects.

If the Brazilian leaderships know how to channel those virtues, when making them to converge for positive ends, while identifying, to neutralize, defects and bottlenecks, South America will then be able to blunt as object of admiration of the other people of the world.

Stock. Which national institutions are good and correct and doesn't Brazilians know how to value?

Many of the Brazilian advantages are affronted because they are seen by many as bales. Others are despised because not even are noticed, at the same time in that poisonous ladies of the night are cultivated as if they were balm.

We will present here a roll of consolidated institutions that need to be valued and defended by Brazilians, instead of suffering gibe and stoning: a) four-year terms, b) government mobility, c) electoral biannuality, d) uninterrupted parliament, e) "compulsory" vote, f) proportional election, g) electoral financing, h) freedom, i) peace, j) official teaching, k) hydro-rail-highway mesh, l) powerful hydroelectrics, m) rich culture, n) sporting capacity, o) cognitive disposition, p) agricultural super park, q) giant wateries, r) mineral wealth, s) climatic diversity, t) exuberant nature.

The items from (a) to (l) have been built through the effort of rulers and parliamentarians, with the support of the civil society. The items (m), (n) and (o) are characteristics of the population, built starting from the settlers' inheritance, of all of the origins. Now the five remaining points, (p), (q), (r), (s) and (t), are gifts of heaven, which indigenous, European, Africans, Semites and Asians here have found, as prize for their trip to this ground.

We show now the meaning and the value of each one of those

points.

Quadrennia. Why are so important the twenty items above?

The period of four years for the government and parliamentary terms was not just drawn in the last years or in the last decades, but it is resulted of those whole centuries in that the democratic system has been improved since Pericles inaugurated it in Ancient Greece. In two and a half millennia of political experience, the humanity learned that the quadrennium is the maximum optimum period. Many rulers, for personal interest, stretch out it, as President Wladimir Putin made in Russia, when changing from four to six years the presidential period. This kind of measure is taken in many places and in several times, but is in force while his author has to be able to guarantee it. France already cultivated presidential mandates of seven years, when having, for instance, President Miterrand during 14 years sat down in the chair of Elisees, because he has been reelected. More ahead, President Sarkozy reduced the period for five years, with possibility of a reelection, which he didn't get to enjoy. Brazil established many decades ago the quadrennial period for the presidency, period disrespected in the Revolution of 1930. The Constitution of 1946 fastened in five years the mandate, and this only came to be altered with the Figueiredo presidency, once President Geisel changed the period of five to six years for their successors. In 1985, President Jose Sarney restored the quadrennial mandate, but in the middle of his administration he converted himself to the quinquennial and made the parliament to approve the return of that model. He was however the only to preside the country for five years from Geisel, because the Constitution of 1988 retook the quadrennial formula. Finally, in 1997, President FHC, after doing to approve dozens of innocuous amendments to the Constitution, with the aim of opening road for his life project, which was the installation of the reelection, made to approve the statute of reelection for the elective executive positions. The politicians, however, need to become aware of the following fact: period larger than four years is too big for a responsible ruler to tolerate, and is also too much time for a country to tolerate an irresponsible chief. The leaders' responsibilities need to be shared, and every wise individual should see that the scepter should be passed to other hands after his valuable democratic contribution as chief of State. Karl Mannheim denominates "contradiction of the democracy" the phenomenon that is observed in the situation in that a ruler receives the news that he was chosen: he, who was theoretically an equal among his pairs before the counting, stops immediately being an equal after being chosen. This is the contradiction: all are equals, but only up the name of the one who stops being equal is revealed. In reelection situation, one among the contestants is had no longer as equal, by nature. Therefore, the device of the reelection for leadership positions is quite antidemocratic. The quadrennial period is a patrimony, which Brazilians need to defend, preferably liberating it of the compromising device of the reelection.

Mobility. Does the rulers' change have great value for the democracy?

The statute of the periodic change of names in the leadership of State is of extreme importance. Such a periodicity is essential for there being social mobility. The systems of breeds only grew in certain societies because the population lived under the regime of the lifelongness of the leadership. If the chief of State could be the same during his complete life, with more reason the social condition of one or other subject should stay unaffected, lifelongly. Just the periodic substitution of the supreme chief, preferentially of quadrennial form, will guarantee in the future the complete abolition of the trace of breeds, in any society in the world. All of the countries that lived under monarchic regimes carry this rancidness in their social relationships. Therefore, it is important that one doesn't underestimate what the United States can give to this respect. The analyses on the theme left by Tocqueville and Stuart Mill, views with foreigner looking, and by Thomas Jefferson, views from within, are valuable.

In Brazil, from the fall of the monarchy, in 1889, only Getulio Vargas, while enchanted with the Fascist regimes in Europe, looked for disrespecting this commitment of the command change in the leadership of State. And even when of his return, elected "by the people", he declared that from the Palace of the Catete he would only leave dead, when UDN urged him to resign, after the murder of major Rubens Florentino Vaz, assistant of Carlos Lacerda, by shot struck by the boss of the president's personal safety, Gregorio Fortunato, as revealed by subsequent investigations. In fact, he left dead the palace when passed away, by suicide, but he left the suspicion that his declaration could mean that he would try to perpetuate in the position, somehow General Franco made in Spain, as remainder of the nazi-fascist years.

It is necessary that Brazilians interpret those pretensions of Vargas as point out of the curve, for valuing with nails and teeth this national patrimony that is the respect to the limit of mandates. And this is not a jabuticaba, an endemic fruit, but a great discovery, vital for all the humanity.

Biannuality. Is it important to respect the regular periodicity of the elections?

From the right final adjustment in the Constitution of 1988, the Brazilian elections were regularized, after a lot of cost, for happening in a biannual way, with municipal elections in leap years, and federal elections in the even no-leap years, always in the month of October. Many politicians who make bet in constitutional amendments to break this regularity see as nonsense the effort that the country did to reach this apprenticeship. In three elections, necessary for the settlement of periods as way to arrive to the biannuality, voting happened for all of the positions in the Republic except the one of president. In a single day of October, in the years of 1982, 1986 and 1988 - and the Brazilian election, when there is not second round, is done in a single day of October, what also means great earnings -, voters suffered in the lines of the electoral sections up to 20h, not up to 17h, as always happen. For it was not easy to vote in a same seating for senator, federal representative, state representative, governor, mayor and town alderman. And this was what the voter did in those elections, which were still handy.

The largest advantage of this biannual regularity is that the voter knows that in every leap year he is called to renew the municipal mandates, and, in the even no-leap years, the mandates of representatives, senators, governors and presidents. If the month of October of an even year to happen and the summons will be not made, the voter will know that something very serious is happening in the political system. Badly comparing, it would be as to arrive in December 25 of any year and to see that the stores didn't present Christmas decoration and that every reference to Santa Claus and the Christmas party was prohibited.

Brazilians need to struggle always to maintain this biannual regularity, which is part of the democratic health, of the little that is had up to now in the country of democratic and citizen normality.

Parliament. Are sound the verbal attacks ordered against the National Congress?

While the voters of the United States are accusing the members of their national parliament of being 'Do-nothing Congress', in Brazil the parliamentarians are also very criticized, but for doing a lot, and very wrong. It is difficult to know what is worse. But the Brazilian critics edge the intolerance. The federal parliamentarians are disrespected and censured as corrupt, independently of deserving or not the accusation. One of the more discussed proposals in the popular circles is the one of the reduction of the number of federal deputies from the current 513 for less than half. And the voters, in great part, simply defend the abolition of the parliament. Yes, while being the presidency of the Republic in the new capital, the institutions are really despised, but the parliament suffers a systematic attack very disproportionate in front of its responsibilities.

The existence of the parliament, in its full operation, for the evil or for the good, is a democracy warranty, even if it is of relative-democracy, as it happened during the military regime in Brazil. The Pinochet regime spared it, in Chile, and in Nazi Germany it just existed as decoration, after some smart one brought for the führer the device of the decree-law.

In the whole history of the Republic in Brazil, the parliament just suffered short periods of interruption. In the military regime, although many parliamentary have been expelled, the National Congress was closed for very short periods, the last time having been in April of 1977, when President Geisel edited the famous 'April package', which introduced some anachronic items, soon discarded, as the imposition of the indicated senator, but this began the disassembling of the military regime itself. When the National Congress was re-opened, one month later, the country was sure that it would pass to live a new era. In fact, ever since, never again the Brazilian parliament was authoritatively closed, and it is waited that never again this comes to happen. If, for misfortune, this expectation comes to be frustrated, Brazilians can be sure that a great political retreat took place.

Parliamentarians need always to be criticized, with responsibility and public spirit. But the parliament has to be respected, and it has to be appreciated by the population as fundamental institution for the warranty of the public freedoms.

Compulsory. Should not we return to the system of voluntary attendance to the urns?

As well as the parliamentarians are severely criticized, one claims a lot also in Brazil against the soft compulsory nature of the vote. The compulsory nature is soft because the fine for the ones who infringe the norm is ridiculous, the cost of one or two coffees, and the punishment for who doesn't regularize the own electoral situation weighs a little on public employees, but is practically non-existent for the workers of the private section. If the voter doesn't exercise his vote, nor justifies his lack, he will be impeded of renewing his passport, while getting not able to travel to the exterior, until to solve his dispute with regard to the electoral tribunal. If he wants to take oath in some public position, he also needs to prove that he voted for in the most recent election. When stopping voting for, no voter will be arrested by this, nor he will stop being primary defendant. The sanction is in fact very small, and it doesn't need to be harder. It just exists as form of pressure. So much it is so that the most popular elections get to take to the urns a maximum of 2/3 of the registered voters, or little more than this.

As some jurists remind, the vote right is not a subjective right, something that the citizen can release when he wants, but a social obligation.

The Brazilian voter is not forced to suffrage any party or candidate. He just has to attend the electoral section, according to the legislation, to sign and to mark his vote, which can be valid, white or null, according to his will.

That compulsory nature was introduced as mechanism of overcoming of the old curse called 'halter vote', in which the colonels took to the urns the voters whom they chose, and these had to vote for on whom they ordered. The compulsory nature for everybody neutralized that power of the colonels. And that power existed, and will exist again, by the fact that Brazilians are not disposed to accomplish their electoral obligation if they will be not submitted the any coercion form. If the compulsory nature is abolished, as some voters want, enchanted with the news that they hear on the electoral models of the United States and France, a first election will count with some 50% of the attendance of the citizens registered to vote for, but in the following elections the number will fall, until stabilizing in the level of the 20%. The only motivation to do this experience totally unnecessary is the habit of imitating, for imitating, any thing that they hear that happens at richer countries. The voluntary voting of those countries is something old and antiquated, as it is in the United States the passion for the schools with fee (they didn't accept Condorcet).

Proportional. Why should not the district vote be restored in Brazil?

The proportional vote is also very criticized by reason very similar to the one of the compulsory vote. The alternative is the district vote, in some cases seasoned as 'mixed-member system'.

In general, except the confirmed conservatives, like Pinochet, who restored the district vote in Chile, the voters who defend this electoral model don't have a clear idea of its operation.

The district vote is the original model of voting, created in Ancient Greece, because nobody had gotten to imagine other. This system is what is in force until today in the United States and in England, but not in Belgium and in Italy.

In this system, the electoral tribunals divide the country in "electoral districts", which are not the regional districts in that the voters live and with which are accustomed. An 'electoral district' is a regional chief's feud. For instance, if Brazil restores this system today, there will be 513 constituencies in the country for effect of voting for the Federal Camera. Each district of those will choose a single representative, the owner of one of the 513 chairs, while discarding all the other contestants of the area. When dividing the number of municipal districts for the number of chairs in the Camera, one sees that, on average, each district will contain 11 municipal districts. In practice, for the population density, some districts will have less than 11 and others will have more than this.

Those regional chiefs, who bite the only available vacancy for his constituency, are in general figures who have some expression in their feud, but nothing besides. The explanation for the nickname of the parliament of the United States, as 'do-nothing Congress', is here. A federal deputy in the system of district vote only becomes politician of expression, state or national, when he is chosen president of the house, or when, for misfortune, he goes by some tragedy, as it happened with nice Gabrielle Giffords, who was shot in an assembly in her district in Arizona.

There are two advantages in that system: the representative's election is cheaper and he is somebody physically close his voters. The advantages close up there, and they are illusory.

When Brazil left that system, in 1946, and chose its first proportional parliament, it took to the Congress National figures as writer Jorge Amado and diplomat Afonso Arinos. Today the parliament is composed by former rectors of universities, former mayors, former governors, writers, actors, musicians, comedians, notable policemen, renowned jurists and many other persons of expression. There are, obviously, many inexpressive representatives, chosen in the vacuum of the coalition votes, or simply in the surplus of the vote handles, but this is the price to pay to have a parliament constituted by important members. Nor all of the famous people have some merit, besides the own fame. Some deputies of the proportional system are in this category. But among all of the varied critics that Brazilians make today to their deputies, none of them includes the fact that they are hidden people, who nobody knows who are, out of the feud that sent them to the parliament.

This is why Brazilian parliamentarians produce too much. And the country just needs to create mechanisms to reduce them in this. They understand that they are paid to create new laws, in amount, and this is resulted of lack of political education in society. The country only needs good laws. Short, simple, effective, but good laws. And in the necessary minimum amount.

As for the proportional vote, it is not something simple of understanding, as it occurs with the district vote, invented in time in that one not at least could dream about the sophisticated arithmetic methods that the electoral tribunals use today in the proportional elections. The model, inspired in ideas of Charles Lennox, 3rd Duke of Richmond, and John Stuart Mill, was presented in book published in Paris in the year of 1870, for the Belgian physicist J. Borely. Belgium was the first country to adopt it, in 1899. When Hitler was chosen, in 1932, for the semi-proportional vote, the new model was ignored by almost everyone. President Hindenburg canceled the elections, indignant with the result, and summoned new dispute, within a much flawed and incipient proportional system (they were 35 electoral districts, electing 28 parties). As he only knew the very old district vote system, the voters went back the urns to choose again... Hitler, who just lowered his number of chairs in the parliament of 37% to 32%, but maintaining relative majority.

Hindenburg gave oath to Hitler in 1933, and, as soon as he died, in 1934, he had his position of president absorbed by the Austrian, who became absolute chief of State and government in Germany.

Campaign. Should the public power to finance integrally the electoral campaigns?

It is strange how the politicians discuss a possible future coming of the public financing of campaigns in Brazil without they to be alerted that this is already a norm, from the Joao Goulart government. In that government it was instituted that the television and radio companies are compensated of the losses of the schedules given in to the electoral advertising of candidates. In practice, the government shoulders the larger part of the expenses of campaigns, which is the payment of the schedules of TV. In the United States, only rich candidates, or those who get good contributions in the market, can make campaign in TV, because there the "free schedule" doesn't exist.

There is also the party fund, which is maintained with public budgets, which finance, inclusively, the parties of very low performance, some of them created only as instruments of crooked deal.

Even so, banks and building site companies spill a lot of money in the campaigns of candidates of their preference. Many politicians want an assumed future public financing to substitute this extra source of resources, without noticing the dimension of the hole that their proposal will cause to the treasure. For the public financing, it is enough the party fund to win a larger substance and the distribution of the budgets among the parties to be more rational. The parties themselves should take charge of the impression of advertising material for candidates, and the expenses with trips (not the aerial ones) should be compensated by presentation of receipts after the election.

Yes, the "free schedule" in TV and radio, guaranteed for the public power, is an excellent democratic patrimony, which Brazilians should defend and never to allow that one or another threaten it.

Freedom. Is Brazil today a country that cultivates freedom?

The Constitution of 1988 consolidated and guaranteed in the

country the respect to the cultivation of the citizenship and the conscience of the value of the usufruct of freedom. Its fifth article, which is part of the stony clauses, which cannot be altered, offers to Brazilians the basic juridical instrument to represent the synthesis of their rights and duties, confirming the political freedom as one of the citizen's most sacred goods.

The right of coming and going, the freedom of expression, the warranty of "habeas corpus", the defense right before the tribunals, the right of political participation, the labor warranties and the universal access to the systems of basic education and health are gains that Brazilians obtained, know well and don't tolerate that one or another wants to subtract them.

However, maintaining such a status demands citizen militancy and perspicacity. Napping in relation to the social conquests is a great risk, in any time and place. For contributing with this is that this chapter was written. If Brazilians are not aware of the progresses that they obtained already, of the advantages that they already dispose, while accepting to throw them out because they imagine that they are cause of inferiority or shame, then the country will never be made possible, while undergoing periodic retreats and making to increase the international distrust on its promises.

An example of healthy institution that Brazilians have is the fact that the police is state, not municipal. If now the policemen present cases of bad conduct, or difficult treating, this is due to the situation of calamity of the basic education system, not to the state model. The municipal guards, which Janio Quadros brought to the country when of his last passage by the city hall of Sao Paulo, they are a recklessness, an immense risk to the warranties of the fifth article. The municipalization is good in certain aspects, but terrible in other ones. With municipal police, a tenth of the adult population of the United States is in the chain. In China, when the tribunals of municipal extent could decree death penalty and execution, the cities attended enormous lines of unhappy persons who underwent the corridor of the death, exactly as the oxen in the slaughterhouses, with the projectiles used for the slaughter being collected of the convicts' families, in a display of how the public power was miserable. Finally, President Hu Jintao signed law restricting to the federal tribunals the prerogative of decreeing death sentence, in one of the largest revolutions of the Chinese history in its walk heading for the civilization. Now president Xi Jinping has been revealing himself as a dogmatic and maybe he doesn't move forward in this politics.

The municipal guards need to be transformed urgently in social workers board and in municipal fire brigades, for all of the conscious mayors, while escaping from the preaching of some salespersons of blood of the television programs of six p. m. This is a necessary road for Brazilians not to throw in garbage basket their freedom so arduously conquered. And the National Congress needs to revoke soon the law that allowed the use of firearms for those guards. One neither can joke with the fascism, nor to open the teeth in front of it.

Peace. Were Brazilian and South American always peaceful?

Today, we lived in harmony in South America. The provincial prejudices, of "green-bellies" against "flat-head", of hill-bills against Bahiensis, of farropillas against maragatos, of Brazilians against Argentineans and of mestizos against Indians are not reasons for civil war, as it has still been happening at Middle East and as it already happened in other centuries in South America itself. We are not naturally peaceful, as in fact no people are it, although lately many persons believe in this. We have political peace because we built it along the history. And the delinquency in the conflicts of the field and in the periphery of the great cities, with growth proportional to that of the progress of uncultured religions <u>and</u> badly drifted (certainly, the church of the reader's parents is better, be which goes), shows that, in their root, the South American people are as violent as any other in the planet.

A history teacher made estimations and she reached the conclusion that of every period of three years, lived by the inhabitants of Brazil before the Republic, two years were of war. This means that we were more warlike than peaceful. Brazil built the peace at the expense of a lot of political transformation, and this is still in course.

For making possible the political organization of South America will mean to delegate to the world the larger example of road of progress for mankind. Brazilians and all of the brothers of the neighborhood need to be alerted as for this.

Schools. Did Brazil have already once a good net of basic teaching?

This author wrote already in several situations and published in book a truth that few people took account: Brazil had the best official school system of the world, until the beginning of the eighties.

He was diversified, yes, because this is natural in every quality process - if everything is strictly similar it is because nothing works - unless one is speaking about electronic apparel of the same series or something of this type. Everybody knows the problem: it didn't contemplate the whole population. A portion too much substantial was out of it.

When the governments decided to enlarge the system for all, then the demagogues and the malicious ones entered field to do the very known damage.

Also the construction of that better school was not a work of mediocre people, nor appeared naturally. Fernando de Azevedo, Anysio Teixeira, Mario de Andrade, Heitor Villa-Lobos, Cecilia Meireles and Darcy Ribeiro are among the intellectuals responsible for the drawing of that complex. They built little by little the school model that came to be approved in the Law of Directresses and Bases of 1961 (LDB-61). And they worked on the model left by Benjamin Constant Botelho de Magalhaes in the beginning of the Republic, with the curriculum mirrored in the basic sciences (Mathematics, Physics, Chemistry and Biology), a patrimony whose immense value the Brazilians need to stop underestimating.

Everybody knows that Brazil is world pentachampion of soccer, but few persons know that the country is also world hexachampion of

Mathematics, with prizes obtained in the International Olympiads of Mathematics, applied to students of the third year of the medium teaching (High School). This is fruit of a time in that the school system was good, and no country of the world arrived close to Brazil in this. Now, under the mythical validity of the demagogic populism, Brazil soon will be left back, outdated for other country, probably Finland or China.

The efforts to rescue the teaching need to be embraced by all. For this it is necessary to go neutralizing the demagogy, until its complete incineration.

Railways. Do the Brazilian railways, hydroways and highways receive the deserved attention?

Brazil had a lot of railways and was walking to have an including rail mesh, to guarantee the progress in several senses. In the Kubitschek government, several projects were canceled, as the one of the Transnortheastern Railway, in order to open space for the road model.

Several times the cheapest and efficient things are not the more adopted. The rail transport is ten times more expensive than the aquatic one, but the road is simply thirty times more expensive than the railway.

However, the country still has a railways' net of big account, although some highways have been destroyed. Only in the last years it is that the governments are retaking the enlargement of this transport model. Railways and hydroways are great development propellers, but the frivolity of many rulers left them in last plan. Many cities of great strength, mainly inside Sao Paulo, were reduced in half, or arrived to almost to disappear, by the abandonment that the country devoted to the railways in the last decades. It is a great wealth, built in other times, but almost totally despised.

Without neglecting of the existent highways, it is necessary to treat with devotion and seriousness the rail system, as well as the hydroways system. And the country has to invest a lot in those areas, while building new ways.

Hydroelectrics. Are hydroelectrics a sound wealth for Brazil?

Brazil doesn't take risk of generating insufficient energy for its demand. Transmission lines are what can lack to take electricity abundantly to all of the points. Instead of spending forces in process against the construction of hydroelectrics, the environmental movement should work so that new power stations of nuclear fission are not built. While the nuclear fusion plants don't make possible, the nuclear projects of fission should be all suspended, and not only in Brazil, because they represent danger without account.

With the construction of the Plant of Itaipu, in the beginning of the seventies, according to the project of the Joao Goulart government, a big natural good was eliminated of the map, the Seven Falls (or Guaira Falls), which was the largest waterfall of the world in volume of water. If the environmental movement was strengthened in that time, maybe it had gotten to impede the work. It was a great loss, but it happened in exchange for the warranty of supply of energy for residences and industries that would not have other substitute except the use of the atomic plants, or the proliferation of the insane thermal plants.

Of course who has horror to the technological progress detests that creation of Nikola Tesla, the hydroelectric, but the contrary campaigns are, most of the time, done with the use of apparels switched in the socket.

Hydroelectrics are, yes, a valuable patrimony, in material and human terms.

Culture. Did Brazil already stand out in the arts some time?

The Brazilian art had its days of glory. From the symphonies of Jose Mauricio Nunes Garcia, in the beginning of the 19th century, to the murals of Portinari and the suites of Villa-Lobos, the world didn't pass far of the Brazilian presence. The golden era, soon buried by the political decisions, was the bossa nova, in its birth. In 2005, an important portal of Internet classified the ten songs more downloaded in the world for cellular phone. Three of them were Brazilian, and all of the fifties: *Road to the Sun*, *The Little Boat* and *The Girl from Ipanema*. Under the Brasilia cost everything deteriorated, although internally few persons have noticed. In 1971, the Reform of the Medium Teaching abolished of the basic gymnasial teaching the subject matter Orpheonic Singing, which Villa-Lobos had gotten to introduce in the national curriculum after a lot of fight, as a way to teach musical theory to all of the adolescents. The intention of the elimination of the matter was that the content was incorporated to the new subject matter Artistic Education, fact that, foreseeably, never happened. In 2009, the National Congress approved the return of the music to schools, but it was victim of an unusual prank. Before proceeding for presidential sanction, ministry of Education made to be worth its position embraced since 1971 and introduced the harmful clause that would transform the project in died letter, in practice: the music would return, in "obligatory way", but as part of the content of Artistic Education. This means that, of the two hundred days of the school year, if the teacher of Artistic Education dedicates one day of class to music, the law is being accomplished.

The subject matter Artistic Education has had just a visible effect from its introduction by the military government: the exhibitions of works of important painters or sculptors, like Picasso and Rodin, get to join lines of kilometers at the doors of the stands. Of rest, the Drawing was already subject matter, before that content. It didn't bring anything besides the formation of those lines and for the country the only way of giving musical formation to its adolescents again, from North to South, is to prohibit the Artistic Education and to approve the Music as obligatory and independent subject-matter, in all of the schools of fundamental teaching.

As for the scenic arts, the actors have good level and the soap operas are sold abroad, while bringing exchange value. But the movies crawl, without great memorable productions, for fault of a still incipient literary cultivation. For having good movies it is necessary to strengthen the literature, but the reading habit still was not built, what does that, of what one sells as literature, little thing survives in quality.

What is had then of advantage in the artistic field? Great potential. If the education gets better again, and the reading habit spreads, the country will win a privileged space in the world artistic scenery.

Sports. Is Brazil really good in sports?

As world pentachampion of soccer, Brazil already reserved its place in the history as for its sporting capacity. The problem is that the other dozens of important sporting modalities have received little attention. In the last times, other Latin-American countries, as well as Portugal, Spain, England and many others, have been producing talents in the soccer in larger proportion than Brazil, while indicating that it is hour of the country to diversify in the diverse sports. Sports cultivated in school, as volleyball and basketball, offer great opportunities. This range needs to increase, and the investment too. Companies have been stopping supplying support, and, therefore, the government cannot neglect the area.

High potential exists, and it was already proven. Just one has to cultivate it.

Talent. Are Brazilians good for learning things?

Someone can think, before the Brazilian students' shameful results in the international tests of the beginning of the 21st century, as the exam of the PISA, of the OECD, that Brazilians have difficulty for learning. These, who are not many, are widely mistaken. Most knows, happily is aware of the problem, that the question concentrates on the deterioration of the education system.

Wasted talents are what is had in profusion lately, since they have studied at bad school, which is synonymous of relaxed school, without commitment with serious evaluation and acquisition of solid knowledge. If the school went an institution driven primordially to sexagenarians, maybe the mechanism of the evaluation went something dispensable, because mature people have notion of their responsibility. In the childhood, the responsibility, for the studies and for other commitments, is something in construction. Educating means developing this sense. The school that starts of the presupposition that children are already responsible by nature, and that, therefore, nobody needs to coerce them (in the more noble sense of the term) to render accounts of their academic dedication, such a school has for plan to destroy their students.

It is necessary to elevate the pattern of the school system, so that Brazilian citizens can be safe.

Farming. Is the Brazilian agriculture late?

Brazil was endowed by the nature of immense agricultural and fish farmer potential. However, the small producers don't receive the support that they need, in most of government's administrations, and the big ones, these are seen as villains by the creators of symbols.

Farmers work with the earth, with the defense of their property (estate) and with the expectation that they will neither be surtax nor confiscated. Then they look for conservative clubs and parties, because the progressive ones find strange those demands. The existence of latifundia is a complication in the relationships of farmers with the remaining of society, but, in theory, the landowner is not the farmer, being in general an heir who is not concerned with production, but with maintenance of his domain. The lunges of the government in the sense of the implantation of the land reform should not threaten the peacefulness of the rural producer who brings new wealth to the country. They owe, yes, to worry the ones who have properties just as jewels, kept under open sky. Besides, a government that intends to solve the agrarian problem in an administration, or in a single generation, doesn't pass of rioter. The problem comes from the Gracchi brothers, in Ancient Rome, and it is not suit to retread the same strategy eternally.

In Brazil, latifundia would not exist today if some decades ago one had taken measures in relation to its transmission, as inheritance or as alienation. It is enough to institute limit of area property for futures proprietors, a thousand hectares, for instance, but not for the current proprietors. The ones who will buy it, they will do this inside the established limit. The ones who will inherit it, receive as property just what is inside the limit, being forced to dismiss the surplus, while selling it. In this case, relatives in first degree should be forbidden of inheriting contiguous areas, so that never they can unite again and to restore the latifundium.

And won't the great producers need larger areas than the one of the established limit? Yes, fortuitously, and in those cases, they should have the entire freedom of leasing lands, in the extensions that they need.

The scientific researches, through the institution Embrapa, brought an enormous increment to the agricultural potential the country already disposed. It is hour of doing the politics to help, instead of disturbing, this economical activity. Do they want to take lands of Indians? They won't take, certainly, lands that are regularized as property of other, be companies, be individuals, be indigenous communities. And if they invent of infringing the law, be accused properly. This will never be the case for most.

The indigenous reservations, however, should not have federal or state roads passing in their interior. If such a thing happens, those families should be moved for just one of the sides of the highway. They who think that to transfer is inhuman should be informed that the Indians are not chained to the area.

While treating the farmers well, Brazil will always be well nurtured, and, therefore, well treaty.

Aquifer. Do we have water for the future?

Brazil already possessed, thankfully, what was considered the largest watery of the world, which is the Guarani Aquifer, shared with Argentina, Uruguay and Paraguay. In 2010, however, scientists identified in the Amazonian what is today had as the largest reservation of fresh water in the world, the Amazon Aquifer (or Alter do Chao Aquifer), which is under the soil of States of Amazon, Para and Amapa.

The risk of contamination for industrial activities has been denounced, mainly in relation to that reservation of more water to the South, and this implicates care that governments have to take, to guarantee the healthy life of the future generations.

If South America takes care well of its watery ones, we will have preserved here what will be able to be the largest natural wealth of the people, which is the drinkable fresh water. In the 19th century, Malthus issued his scream against a possible crisis of alimentary provisioning. Today we know that the larger risk is in a possible crisis of water supply.

Brazilians need to look with pride, but also with a lot of affection, their reservations of water.

Ores. Does the mineral wealth still represent a good potential?

The mineral wealth of Brazil is well known. From the times of the colony, the taming of the interiors occurred almost exclusively because of the search of diamond, gold, silver and precious stones. The more the prospectors went obtaining results, more they penetrated the forests and more the country went being discovered and peopled.

In the last times, those ores of high value no longer are very abundant, so that the larger exploration of the underground is in the extraction of the iron, to supply the industries of China, more than the ones of Brazil, which are being shrunk from the beginning of the eighties.

The petroleum, whose era was almost in its death rattles, has received a great encouragement with the exploration of the pre-salt, under the sea. It is an immense wealth, but with period of very certain and short validity. Brazilians need to know how to take advantage of it.

Anyway, Brazil has valuable ores, which are a great patrimony, and on them it is necessary to apply the best politics.

Climate. Is the climatic diversity a negative point to Brazil?

Frost in the Gaucho Mountain in June and scalding sun in the Plateau of Araripe in December. Humid winds, hot winds, hurricanes, low humidity of the air, high humidity of the air, hail, torrential rains and big periods of drought: Brazilians are accustomed to this climatic diversity and have been learning how to live together with it along the centuries.

It is right that the country still lacks of good preventive politics, mainly as for the floods and as for its opposite, the droughts. Rigorous inspection so that residences are not built in risk areas is a demand of the most pressing. And, as for the drought, it is not far in the horizon the day in that it will stop being problem: weir-dams for all of the susceptible cities and efficient systems of irrigation are the works the population needs.

With the necessary investments, the climatic diversity of the country will only be able to be seen as a wealth.

Nature. Does Brazil still count with great natural wealth?

The tourism has not been yielding the Brazilians everything that its potential promises for fault of the problem that generates the disease of the currency, which is the same that generates the bad education and, in consequence, the rude treatment that the foreigners receive of certain portion of citizens, including the criminals there. Without the "Brasilia cost", Brazilians could make a lot of money with the tourist activity, because the nature was excessively generous to the country. The exuberance of beaches is unquestionable. The diversity of the fauna and the flora, accessible for trips along Rio Negro and Amazon River, is reason of charm for all of ones who are disposed to spend more than the reasonable to visit those areas. Big tablelands, thousands of waterfalls, and even a desert, formed by the Lencois Maranhenses, are at the disposition of visitors, be external, be domestic.

Brazilians will spend vacation in Northern Hemisphere because they discover that it is much more expensive to travel inside the own country.

If the larger bottleneck will be expired, if the life will be cheaper for the tourist, if the exchange comes to be favorable, the nature will be the largest allied of Brazilians in the field of the hostelry industry and of the tourism.

5. On politics

Government. Is the chief of State, while accumulating government's leadership, a sound politics?

When in the Republic the chief of State also exercises the position of chief of government, one has what was stipulated to call presidentialism. There are several inconveniences in this device.

With the death of the president of Germany, the chief of government, Hitler, accumulated the leadership of State, as it was already said above. If he was a man of less unhealthy Messianism, he would have coordinated the election of the successor of Hindenburg, or, in the case of not having really how to escape to the calling, he would have become president and provided the indication of a successor as chancellor (premier). One should be notice that this political model, apparently invented in the United States, is not something usual in Europe.

Thomas Jefferson, who took the fault by the formulation of the concept of presidentialism, didn't have intention of creating this that came being formed as snowball and became the so-called presidentialism nowadays. In his project, the function of governing the United States should fall to the governors. The president of the union should have the role of representing the federation, with "a very small body of employees". If it was to he to govern, he would have a ministry, not a group of secretaries. Obviously, as the country strengthened a lot, one demanded of the president the task of involving in several typical actions of rulers.

The countries of Latin America copied the system without taking into account the concern of Jefferson as for the preservation of the federalism, i. e., without taking care for the detail that the role of governing should belong to the chiefs of state executives.

So, the presidential system of Latin America, with strong president, while governing in almost all of the fronts and in almost all the themes, aided by a ministry, is a counterfeit, which didn't emerge from the feather of any theoretical one. It appeared from an accommodation and a copy badly done of the model of the head office, which no longer accomplished the role originally drawn.

Parliamentarism. Should then Brazil become parliamentarist?

In the new campaign for the implantation of the parliamentarism, which would happen on April 21, 1993, in the plebiscite that resulted in the confirmation of the presidentialism, as victory of Brizola, by the second time in his life, and of Roberto Marinho, circumstance allies, in that campaign Mr. Ulysses explained because he supported the clause of limitless reelection for president. He said that once the parliamentarism was adopted, the country would have to accept all the built-in practices in that system. In his mind, reelection per times without account was an intrinsic component.

Finally, Brizola and Roberto Marinho convinced the voters and the parliamentarism didn't return. This author and a greater portion of supporting of the parliamentarism were relieved with that defeat, because the victory would implicate to carry all of the defects that the political leaderships judged of obligatory implantation, while being the most terrible that of the limitless reelections. Now, those politicians didn't notice that the one that they saw as elements inherent to the system were, in the reality, retrograde pieces, defects that the parliamentarist countries still had not gotten to repair.

The plebiscite, in fact, in the two editions in that it happened, was lost beforehand, because of the way as the question was asked. It wondered "parliamentarism, yes or not", and this was the same as to ask "integral of analytical functions, yes or not". The voter had to vote for in the code that the leadership of larger credibility ordered, without having idea of what he was doing. So much that, a few days after the heavy defeat of the parliamentarism in 1993, an informal popular survey with the question "the president should direct Brazil aided by a prime-minister, yes or not", of absolutely clear meaning for any literate citizen, it gave as result 82% of "yes". And before the accomplishment of the plebiscite, other informal survey revealed that among the freshmen of the medium teaching students the preference for the parliamentarism was of 25%. This number was growing linearly until that, among the freshmen of the university, the parliamentarism had 75% of preferences.

Today, some decades elapsed, only few parliamentarist countries maintain the statute of the presidential reelection for infinite times. The mechanism of the dissolution of the parliament, without respecting the quadrennial period, has been reviewed in several democracies. Some items that the Brazilian politicians judged exclusiveness of the presidentialism were, truly, neutral progresses, which should be adopted in any system.

Yes, every serious country should work for the implantation of the parliamentarism. But instead of foreseeing the dissolution of the parliament as way of overcoming crises, the wiser is to create vice-premier positions, at least about three, first vice, second vice and third vice. Most of the crises that seem insoluble can be solved with the change of the leadership, simply.

What an (imperceptible) happiness a substitution of Hitler for a judicious vice-premier, before the death of Hindenburg, would have been for the world? The president could have used one of the chancellor's harsh and rough measures, as, for instance, the exclusion of the Jews of the public service, for creating a noisy crisis, with good purposes, and then to proceed to the defenestration of that nut. The world would never come to know the debt of gratitude that it should have to the president.

Some advantages of the parliamentarism can be reminded here: (1) the party that wins most of the chairs, which is the really winner party, receives the incumbency of forming the government - he who wins governs -, liberating the country of the very common situation in the presidentialism in that a president wins the election for conducting soon the government against a hostile parliament; (2) the division among two people of the command of the country is a warranty against coup d'état, although not absolute; (3) the chief of State is preserved of businesses that can commit the State itself, while being able to cultivate a breeze of purity, except by the past life; (3) the premier change is much less traumatic than the one of president in moments of crisis; (5) a possible presidential resignation doesn't affect the conduction of the government, as one can see by comparing the resignation of Janio Quadros in Brazil, in 1961, with the resignation of President Horst Koehler in Germany, in 2010, for refusing to sign the sending of new troops to Afghanistan.

The parliamentarist system, used by Hitler as stairway and later trampled by him, is the sound option so that we can install the more functional possible type of government.

Election. Is there some insoluble problem in the model of presidential direct election?

The neuralgic point of this book is here. At the beginning, it is important to inform that the author was an enthusiast of presidential direct election, up to 1973.

Before the coup of 1964, direct election or election by council were indifferent methods to the author. But the coup left the impression that, if the conservatives avoided the direct election, it is because it should be good: reasoning for reverse effect. Under the first times of the most dictatorial quinquennium of the military regime, which was the Medici presidency, this impression was stiller reinforced. But we cannot just look at our own navel. It is necessary to see Western Europe, Russia, North America, Asia and other areas.

The report of the direct election should be taken into account by they who continue in its defense.

With inspiration in ideas of Rousseau, Robespierre tried to introduce the model, but he was guillotined before having time of rendering his plan.

After some progress and many retreats, France lived in 1848 one almost entire year of revolution, with the first Communes of Paris. In the month of November, to put a term to the days that had been begun in February, the political leaderships got right a direct election to the presidency. That was consensus practically, before the exhaustion of those months of fight, and this seemed a salvation board. Minus for a group, the one of the historical materialism, which came participating actively of the shocks. The leaderships of this group, as one knows, were people arising from Germany, England and even Cuba, but with few people from France. Their alerts didn't have repercussion on that moment, although their prophecies came to show themselves well aimed.

When the direct votes were counted, suddenly was chosen nobody less than Napoleon's nephew, Louis Bonaparte, a born activist of coup. It is not that most noticed this. He went governing, convincing, until that the time came in that he would have to prepare the passage of the position to other. On December 2, 1851, Charles Louis Napoleon Bonaparte closed the parliament and brought the coup, while transforming France again in imperial regime, governing from then as Napoleon III.

It was like this the experience of the first direct election to the presidency in a big and important country.

Example. Even so, does France recognize Louis Bonaparte's republican presidency?

The shame by that fiasco settled among the French historians and among the organizers of the ceremonial of the presidency of the Republic themselves. Louis Bonaparte is not the man worshipped as the first president of France. The first president, officially, is Louis Adolphe Thiers, elect by the parliament in 1871, after the Franco-Prussian War and the consequent fall of the emperor.

On those times, the mirror of Brazilians was not still Yankee America, but France. It is so that, some years later, Don Pedro II was dethroned and the Republic was installed. The first President, marshal Deodoro da Fonseca, arrived to the position by parliamentary election, as well as marshal Floriano Peixoto who succeeded him after resignation, however already in the following election, in 1894, Brazil not followed France of then, but the one of 1848, because the electoral process was direct, resulting in the victory of Prudente de Morais. The system, which is predestined to the disaster, was in force up tol the Revolution of 1930.

The direct method, retaken by the Constitution of 1946, chose marshal Eurico Gaspar Dutra (1946), Getulio Vargas (1950), Juscelino Kubitschek (1955) and Janio Quadros (1960). Of the 23 presidents, of complete mandates or not, between that Vargas of 1930 and President Dilma Rousseff of 2010, eight of them were chosen directly to the presidency. As the method seems to be consolidated, in spite of the first chosen directly after the military regime to have gone by congressional deposition, Brazilians tend to trust the process, because President Dilma Rousseff is already the third titular of the position who doesn't suffer mandate interruption (up to 2014), while completing two decades in apparent institutional peacefulness, after the FHC and Luiz Inacio presidencies. The responsible for this "miracle" is not other that the plan of monetary stabilization, of 1994. But, as it was proven in the days of June 2013, the country has a highly expensive stabilization, for being very fragile. The inflationary pulse, great villain of Brasilia, was just anesthetized, while being able to wake up at any moment.

Cleavage. Is not the presidential direct election used at the best countries?

The club of the Republics that maintain in this beginning of millennium the method of the presidential direct election has a common characteristic, except South Korea, which copied the French model in 1990: those countries are Republics of Cassock. Some are formed under Catholic cassocks, be Roman, be orthodox. Other are formed under the black cassocks of the mullahs, like Afghanistan, Indonesia and Iran (in fact, this country, not North Korea, lives the worst imaginable political situation today, with its supreme chief, for life theocratic, in the Versaillist city of Qom). In the case of the Shiite Republics, the populations have science today that they live under theocratic regime. In the case of the Catholic ones, the citizens live in a world of permanent rebelliousness in relation to the Church, but suffering in their flesh the effects of the negative portion of the religious formation to that they renounce. The good and positive aspects of the Catholicism are cultivated and enjoyed by few persons. The most harmful trace, which is this that makes the citizen to enchant with the presidential direct election, is not, nor from a distance, seen as a problem. However, the presidential direct election is the great Catholic-Shiite disease today.

Just Cuba, whose government lives a transformation process inside the philosophy of the materialism, and Italy, on the other side of Atlantic Ocean, are countries of Catholic formation that escape now from the destiny of Republics of Cassock. The reason so that Italy escapes is due to a pathetic figure: Benito Mussolini. The years that Italy lived under this deceiver leader has left it vaccinated against the demagogy and the populism, although he has never been chosen directly as President.

And in the years of 2013 and 2014 the world attended amazed to the delivery of Egypt to the inebriating enchantment of the directism, after to drop and to imprison its very brief first elected demagogue.

Fallacious. And as for the positive things what do they say on the presidential direct election?

A harmful system could not last decades, as it has happened in Mexico during one century, if a group of ennobling lies was not built. Practically everything that is said of advantageous in the directism is lie or illusion. What is the direct election?

1. Federalist? No, each man is a vote in the chief, soon it is unitarist.
2. Cheap? No, it is the more wasteful model of election.
3. Pro-parliament? No, it erodes the parliament and leads it to crooked deals.
4. Participative? No, it is mythicizer, because candidates come from the summits.
5. Progressive? No, it is demagogic and drops the countries that adopt it.
6. Educational? No, it is destructive of the quality of the education system.
7. Superior? No, it is the system of the mediocrity.
8. Perennial? No, only in Mexico it has some longevity.
9. Safe? No, it is the game of the jump in the darkness.
10. Laic? No, it is the pseudolaicity of the Republics of Cassock.

Mexico, only country that passed one century in practice of the direct election, serves as example of how the system delays society, because Mexico is beside the United States, the richest country in the world, separate by a poor-rich segregation wall, having been formed at the same time, on an indigenous society very much more advanced than the ones of the United States and Canada. Basically two aspects guaranteed that longevity: prohibition of reelection and indication of candidates among the government cadres better accepted by the voters. Max Weber, who explained the "capitalism" as a result of the Protestant ethos, interpreted the precedence of the religion correctly among the social facts, but he didn't explore the interface that takes from the religion to the economy, which is the politics properly. Mexico could have equivalent per capita income to the one of the United States if it had other electoral model, even being Catholic country, as the highly developed Luxembourg.

Mexico never produced scientific cadres at the height of an Irene Joliot-Curie, the French who demonstrated the possibility of the fission of the atom. But France is not a Republic of Cassock? Yes, but in the first half of the 20th century, when people like Luc Montagnier and Pierre-Gilles de Gennes were formed, both of 1932, there was not direct election, system that was exhumed by general De Gaulle, for the Constitution of 1958. Ever since, France and Mexico competed by the anti-science, but in November of 2009 France was saved by the European Union, whose president is chosen by the chiefs of government. Now what is waited is that the European Union gets rid of the Versailles-Weimar Effect, brought by the installation of the presidency of the European Council in Brussels.

Populism. The populism is not a good path for the politics?

The populism, a few persons noticed, is the Latin-American version of the fascism. While in Italy and Germany the fascist leaders used the parliament to arise to the command positions, in Latin America the road would have to be the presidential direct election, for the construction of the same ideals.

Bertolt Brecht recommended with vehemence that intellectuals avoided the word "volk" (people), because the fascists of all the shades abused that term. In Portugal, the Salazarism imposed that the word was written with uppercase 'P'.

The root of the populism is this cultivation of the "people" as mystic entity, the same root of the nazi-fascism.

The nazi-fascism is a movement of demagogues who deceive and seduce the left and center-left parties for later give their heads in the tray, as Herod did with John the Baptist to assist Salome. This dancer, Salome, is the representation of the conservative anti-liberal hosts.

While knowing that conservatism and right-wingism are the political tendencies that ignore or reject the fight for the improvement of the conditions of the poor life, it is necessary that the voters know how to distinguish the two basic types of left: on a side, the progressive democratic left, and, of other, the crypto-fascist left, cultivator of both the acception of persons and the violence, some times explicitly, other times in latent forms, with authoritarian inclination and for life pretensions.

In this point, other rude lie of the politicians and intellectuals from Latin America needs to be denounced. It consists of teaching the youths that nazi-fascism and right-wing are a same thing. Now, the climbers that use the left to guarantee their ascension and later to form an alliance with the conservative parties act in the same way that fascists of Europe in other time, who had for forming Mussolini the Italian socialism, for forming Hitler, the national-socialism, old "Deutsch Arbeiter Partei", and for Franco, in Spain, the national-syndicalism. Those Latin-American leaderships cultivate the populism. They survive mounted in this lie: nazi-fascist is the other, the individual of the right wing, or classic liberal.

Now, who is classic liberal, or of the right wing, without being opportunist conservative, is heavy enemy of the fascism. In the hard years of the fight against the military regime, the liberals formed an alliance with the lefts in the same old Brazilian Democratic Movement (MDB), against the conservatives who used the military men in their benefit. Many liberals were inside the military government initially, like Teotonio Vilela and Severo Gomes, but little by little the things went being explained and they closed lines on the correct side. There is even the case of Professor Antonio Delfim Netto, Keynesian and Fabian, who served to the regime in two different terms and continued in the party of the dictatorship (PP: "Progressive" Party), being chosen deputy later, only entering much later the MDB. The case of the President Jose Sarney is a special case. Convinced by the leader of the old MDB, Mr. Ulysses Guimaraes, and by others of the party of the opposition, to abandon the party of the dictatorship, of which he was president, and to ally to the opposite side, to guarantee the transition (and, finally, to lead it), he was chosen as vice president in election by parliamentarians and he had to head the leadership of State, once the title-holder Tancredo Neves died on the eve of what would be the day of the oath. If Sarney went a demagogue shaver, he would have included in the election of 1986, when he was with 96% of popular approval, a referendum that confirmed his mandate. As parliamentary, he was always vigilant. As a registration, in the second year of the Dilma Rousseff presidency a senator wanted to give her a supposed present in the daytime of Women, while destroying without knowing the device of CLT (Consolidation of the Laws of Job) that bans payment of different wages for man and woman in the same function. It would start there to be just a small fine to the offenders. This author informed the president of the Senate, Sarney, and immediately he blocked the measure, with help of Senator Romero Juca. In any of his performances, however, Sarney was victim of slanders, always accused of being blamed by the poverty of his State, Maranhao.

Of course the military regime disentangled of the populism, because its plan was to present other perspective to the conservatives, who no longer trusted a lot in the demagogues. But populism and conservatism, finally, are only two faces of the same retrograde coin.

Super-father. Should the population trust life long leaders?

The countries that create populists are not just harmed themselves. Austria, Republic of Cassock, which before was part of the Austro-Hungarian Empire, formed the most terrible demagogue of all of the times, and exported him to Germany: Adolf Hitler.

Those countries, therefore, don't just nourish the voters that look for the father-of-the-poor, while dreaming about the direct election for electing him then. Those voters are, in their majority, in search of that figure of sweet speech and bitter heart. And the existence of voters formed in this way is a tragedy itself.

But as serious as this voter type to exist is the father-of-the-poor in formation to exist, because he is not the deceived, he is the magician, the illusionist who knows how to take advantage of the good will and credulity of the poor.

The progress of the society is a collective construction, and no man can want to give himself to the luxury of saving homeland anywhere in the world. Many persons complained Mandela, for he not being the promoter of the social elevation of the South Africans, without noticing that the role that he gave himself was this of accomplishing the transition of the segregationist regime to the political democracy, in the one that he was impeccable. It will fit to other ones, and many others, to embrace the fight for the improvement of the material conditions of the life of the population. And it has to be so, without anybody wanting alone to hug the world, because every candidate to father-of-the-poor, be similar to Hitler, Mussolini, Peron, Vargas, Salazar, Janio Quadros or Ferdinand Marcos, needs to be rejected for who has condition for this.

Unviableness. Is Brazil viable as a political entity?

Brazil, as a political entity, is not a viable country. Who said "Brazil is viable" was marshal Artur da Costa e Silva, after sitting down in the presidential chair in 1967. With the time, he must have noticed that he made a hurried evaluation.

Obviously, the territory is viable and the population is viable. What is not? The political entity Brazil. What are the indications of this? They are countless. Without a hierarchical order, we pointed some of them here.

In 1960 Brazil inaugurated a new capital officially built in the middle of the bush, among the corrals, with magnificent cement plans, around a great artificial lake. This would be even justifiable if the country was not abandoning the more beautiful city of the world in exchange for that.

In 1808 Don John VI docked in Bahia, while escaping from Napoleon Bonaparte's troops, with intention of doing of Brazil the headquarters of the United Kingdom of Brazil, Portugal and Algarves (it was recommendation done by Priest Vieira two centuries before). As the administration had already been installed years before in the city of Rio de Janeiro, Don John VI steered there with his cortege to install the court. His idea was "to tame" the city to turn it capital of a great kingdom, without knowing at that time that this would take more than one century. He didn't bear it. Contempt on the part of the subjects in Brazil, beginning of revolution being established at the Portuguese city of Oporto, the roughness and the hell produced by the Ravenna Effect, all this took him to return to Lisbon, in April of 1821, while leaving in Brazil his son Pedro, to take care of the territory that returned to the colony condition.

If it was not easy for Don John VI taming the wild tiger called Rio de Janeiro, either it was to his son. From April 26, 1821, to April 7, 1831, day of the Regency, when he returned to Portugal, his life in Brazil was to fight. Revolutions and separatists wars cracked from North to South, with victories and reverses that would not be so current if they were not being stimulated by the new capital.

With the coup of the majority, copied of Russia, Don Pedro II had his majority declared when he completed 14 years old, and the period of the Regency was then finished. Don Peter II was crowned on July 18, 1841, and Brazil hoped to enter an era of peace. However, the tiger was not calmed down still. After many minor conflicts set up, the emperor had to face, 23 years after the coronation, the largest war already fought in the history of South America, which was the Paraguayan War, happened between 1864 and 1870. Many fascists who are always repeating that it misses to South America a great bloodbath, to mature the "character" of the "people", certainly never stopped to think of what that massacre represented.

When the Republic was proclaimed, in 1889, with the consequent deportation of the Orleans and Braganca family to Europe, the domestic conflicts were reduced, but the country still had to pass for the War of Canudos and for the period of economical crisis called "girthing", a rural name for "pressure".

Suddenly, when less it was waited, Rio de Janeiro was consecrated as capital. It ripened and started to favor the country. The introduction of the musical subject-matter of Villa-Lobos, the creation of the bossa nova and the shine of Pele in Sweden were fruits of that tree that, finally, allowed profitable vintage.

Then a presidential administration resulting of unhealthy process, the presidential direct election of the abjured Republics of Cassock, decided to build another capital, and to throw the country in the cage of the furious lion. The Army accepted the incumbency of taming it in 1964, but the weapons of the Army were for another thing.

Finally, that systematic disrespect to what the ancestors built, at the expense of a lot of blood, as it was the case of the consolidation of the more beautiful city of the world as capital of the country, this disrespect and this contempt are a first display that Brazil is unviable. This pulse was not an imposition of that man, who just removed it of the profundities of the population's dark basement of the unconscious. Otherwise, it would be enough to convince the country that the leader was wrong, and everything would be repaired.

Signs. Why do some persons say that Brazil passes as if it was invisible?

It is not the fact of the country to have built a new capital that proves its unviableness. This is just one among many indications. When the path was shown, rulers preferred "to shoot the trouble", with the plan of stabilization that fans the breath of the dragon, instead of exterminating the monster.

As was said in the "Estigma de Pindorama", there is no rejection to the territory, but to the symbol. The words "Brazil" and "Brasilia" and the Brazilian flag are symbols of oppression in the humanity's unconscious.

One day Brazil will win Nobel, of Literature, for instance. This won't be a sign that the country is viable ("and a certain author was wrong"), but that the Academy decided to feel sorry for this country that so many times enrolled authors and had never been assisted.

One day Brazil will win Oscar. The reason of the prize in the Academy of Hollywood will be the same used in the Academy of Stockholm.

Therefore, it is of good prudence that Brazil looks for reformulating, before being honored just because they felt pity.

Some persons will say: one day Brazil would win a saint, and it won: Saint Anthony Galvao. Yes, but they should not ignore the fact that the Holy Seat treats of the things that are not of the kingdom of this world. To the kingdom that is not of this world, countries don't exist, souls exist.

Being a country hated by others is something more preoccupying than to be an unknown country. And a hated country suffers many times warlike attack of its disaffections. Would the case be of not warming up mind with the Brazil's displays of invisibility in the exterior? It would be, but only if this didn't go a demonstration that the country is unviable. Let us see some cases.

A) *Balloon*. Roger Bacon described the balloon of hot air in England, in the 13th century, but the first person to build the apparel and to elevate it of the ground was the born in Santos Brazilian Priest Bartolomeu de Gusmao, in Lisbon, in the year of 1709. The recognition, however, falls to the Montgolfier brothers, in invention of 1783.

B) *Airplane*. Santos Dumont discovered the vertical propulsion of the motors in 1906 and, with this, he created the airplane with takeoff.

Before, this was impossible. But the Wright brothers registered the patent of the airplane in the United States in 1903. It is right that it worked by catapult, not for takeoff, but the patent that is worth for the world is the one of them, what guarantees them the primacy. Before, the dirigibleness of the balloons was developed by the Paraensis pilot Julio Cesar Ribeiro de Sousa, with his balloon "Santa Maria of Belem", in July of 1884, primacy that is not recognized internationally up to today.

C) *Ethanol.* The combustible alcohol, for automobiles, was resulted of the Program of the Alcohol, Pro-alcohol, 1974. It was a slow and very costly process, which involved almost the whole Polytechnic School, the Institute of Technological Researches and at least half of the College of Economy and Administration of the USP (University of Sao Paulo). However, somebody published that Henry Ford tried in the beginning of the 20th century three types of fuels, alcohol, Diesel and gasoline, while having opted for this last one for the low cost. Now, the United States consider that the father of the combustible ethanol is nobody less than Henry Ford.

As for Priest Roberto Landell de Moura, had as inventor of the radio, in 1899, in Sao Paulo, it is done necessary to publish an important information: the patent now recognized to the radio is of Nikola Tesla, 1897, no more the one of Marconi.

Also the fact that USP has left the roll of the first two hundred universities of the world in 2013, in the Times Higher Education classification (THE) of England, doesn't mean that the world made the arbitrary decision of turning invisible Brazil in the academic extent. The problem was internal and it was due exclusively to the destruction of the basic teaching. In certain moments, many persons presented as contradiction the fact that Brazil has a horrible basic teaching and an academic teaching of high level, internationally recognized, without noticing that this "horrible basic teaching" was resulted of bad politics and that it would necessarily drop the academic excellence of the universities in the course of time. There was not any contradiction, just histeresis, the phenomenon that makes an effect to maintain during some time after having interrupted its source.

In the turning of the century the Latin American universities in that classification were two: the Autonomous University of Mexico and the USP. For the same reasons that the Brazilian case, the Autonomous went down before. Finally, no university of the area is listed. The USP and the Unicamp (University of Campinas) are still among the first four hundred, but they take the risk of going down more.

Defects. Are the Brazilian defects easily corrigible?

Brazilians have their many virtues and advantages, but these can be neutralized by the defects, if these don't suffer the necessary load of attacks that will transform them in domesticated animals. The main defects, with the names of the ones that identified them - even judging them quality -, proceed below.

1. Frivolity (Michael Kepp)
2. Iconoclasty (Oswald de Andrade)
3. Dilapidation (Jose Honorio Rodrigues)
4. Diplomism (Afonso Henriques de Lima Barreto)
5. "Accusaltrism" (Eduardo Giannetti da Fonseca)
6. Monkeyishness (Jose Marti)
7. "Misopatry" (Antonio Carlos Jobim)
8. Ergophobia (Gilberto Freyre)
9. "Exam-cheatism" (Dolores Sala)
10. Arithmophobia (Mario Henrique Simonsen)

The list above is not in gravity order, but mnemonic convenience, because it forms the acrostic Fiddammeea. It is necessary to comment on some of those defects. The Frivolity is something widespread, but very identifiable in some characteristics that the US-American reporter Michael Kepp identified in the Brazilian behavior, mainly the incapacity of saying "not", while preferring to leave the other "in the hand", and the old habit of arriving late. The "Accusaltrism", habit of accusing others without proof, or projecting in the other the own defects, is a disturbing element of the good coexistence among Brazilians, which needs to be treated in the educational process. The Monkeyishness, that before in Portuguese was "macaquice", term whose use became politically incorrect, since Argentinean soccer fans mixed everything, while thinking that it was blemish of ethnic aggression, is very harmful in the measure in which the Brazilian politicians have the habit of copying nonsense of all of the important countries - and even of very small and badly governed countries, as the device of the vote of the 16 years old copied of Nicaragua by Representative Francisco Rossi -, while disturbing the copy of the good measures and practices, which pass getting confused with the mere cultural colonization. It is not possible to build a conduct of pride without giving up this submissive habit of copying nonsense. The "Misopatry", horror to the homeland things or to the compatriots themselves, comes from long time. So that Brazilians watch the works of the national movies is done necessary to approve law of "quotas" (who wants to know what "quotas" make, should read W. E. Deming). For leading them to buy national products, sometimes very superior to the imported of the same category, is necessary to approve laws of the national similar. What sense does it make, for instance, to buy trains of Spain and France when the Brazilian engineering is today superior to the one of those two countries? For it is so. The contempt for the homeland products is so big that the country no longer has factories of trains. If a Brazilian blunts, soon he becomes victim of his compatriots, who, instead of envying him, if don't want to admire him, simply start to hate him. Antonio Carlos Jobim said: "Making success in Brazil is an insult". The horror to the culture of the merit (HCM) is so ingrained that, if somebody ascends, soon it comes the suspicion that he got his position for excused means. Many persons get to arise for own merits, in spite of everything, but they are target of distrust, because most doesn't know what is merit. The Brazilian super-talents have to be prepared very early to face the destructive envy, the spite and the contempt of the part of their compatriots. Carlos Chagas, Osvaldo Cruz, Villa-Lobos, Luiz Gonzaga, Pele, Jobim, Ayrton Senna and several others had to pass their difficulties of coexistence inside the country.

Innovation. From where does the resistance to the domestically produced innovation come?

During 2,500 years Brazil, then Pindorama, was colonized by the Tupis, a strayed branch from the Inca, who went up the Andes and came walking to spread for the oriental coasts of South America. It is supposed that they were Indians who didn't accept any innovations that could happen among theirs, being this probably the reason of the migration to a so distant place. Dispersed for Pindorama, the ethnic group Tupi established the code of the rejection to the innovation, as way of building a civilization rid of the conflict caused by the social mobility. Wars always existed, but they came because of honor. All of them were equal in the condition of men of the Neolithic, when Europe already produced cannons, great caravels, windmills, pens, compasses, mirrors, stained glass windows, swords and fine woven. The life of Tupis limited to hunt, fish, fight, practice ritual sports, paint patterns, build hollow, weave baskets and cook ceramic, always in the same repeated molds during centuries. Somebody who brought some innovation, even if it was some technique of counting until six, was ridiculed quickly, excluded of the conviviality of his companions. That is not such an unusual way of life, because, in the old world, Joseph, son of Jacob, was sold as slave by his brothers to merchants who went to Egypt, just because he was more talented than the others of the house and, later, as administrator of that country, *"prime minister avant la lettre"*, he ordered to get up and to register that whole history. In Pindorama, any Joseph who appeared would have to suffocate his creative lines and inclinations, as condition to continue accepted in the tribe. Starting from 1498, when Duarte Pacheco Pereira, John Ramalho and Americo Vespucio started to explore the coasts that today form Brazil, Tupis discovered that there were human beings with other degree of development in their way of life and they started to see them as people endowed with extraordinary powers. It was so that pioneer Bartolomeu Bueno deceived a whole tribe, while setting fire in a bottle gourd of liquor and threatening to do that with all of the waters of the rivers and lakes.

The result was that the innovation capacity became accepted, but it would have to come from other people. Inventions of the ones who were born in the Brazilian territory continued to suffer of the same contempt that they were already suffering there was more than two millennia. Homeland talents continued to be depreciated. Also the monkeyishness comes from this. As the country cannot innovate, but he needs to accompany the evolution of the people, it remains to copy from foreigners, even any nonsense.

Work. Does Brazil devote respect to the manual labor?

The horror to the manual work (HMW) comes from time very different from that of the horror to the innovation. Tupis were diligent manual workers and they would not be the responsible for leaving this harmful mark in the Brazilian life. The problem was built in the colony and in the reign, stressed with the period of the slavery.

Playing a packing paper in the ground and to lower to catch it, while taking it to the garbage can, is a habit cultivated in Brazil only by very well trained people, in education terms, in the wide sense, not only in the one that concerns to the learning of the grammar and counts.

Of course the noblemen, and the owners of slaves, in their golden times of colony and reign, had slaves at their disposal to clean any dirt thrown to the ground. All those who were not owners of slaves, but that aspirated to be it, saw in that type of privilege something to be reached. This is why today Brazilians of any social segment dirty their spill hoping others come to do the cleaning, same knowing that no longer there is slavery. They wait that somebody without being slave, but being subordinate, come to accomplish that role.

In the basic schools, of gymnasium level, the subject matter Manual Works was introduced in the Capanema Reform in 1942 and it lasted until the Reform of the Medium Teaching, of the military regime, in 1971, with extinction implemented in 1973. Those three decades of cultivation of the subject matter were an imposition that the Brazilian middle class didn't accept to swallow, and came to rid of it in the first opportunity. It didn't go by the mind of those anachronic apprentices of owner of slaves that the learning of the manual works represents cultural and biophysical enrichment for all of the human beings, while serving as base for the poor to enterprise activities and as source of splendid human knowledge for the children of the high classes. How do they want to have in their family a good doctor if this didn't get ability to handle the bistoury, for not having workout in the last years of the fundamental course the handling of scissors, square, compass, hammer, handsaw, line and needle? The one that the middle class wanted, finally, at least the rude middle class, was the ignorance in relation to the work.

That middle class doesn't know that the gymnasium learning of the Manual Works, at least for one or two years, is constituted in the largest device against the juvenile nihilism that takes to the delinquency and the suicide. For this reason, the country retrograded from the well-known light-hand ones of the sixties, the pickpockets produced by the job lack and by the high inflation of that time, to the unhappy authors of armed robberies who act in almost epidemic level in the beginning of the 21st century. The first year without Manual Works, 1974, was the year of the creation of the Febem (foundation of the teenager welfare), the house of boys "in conflict with the law".

Until some years ago, in the 20th century, Brazilians were respected at other countries as hard-working people. In the last times, the laziness and the fraud became curse among the Brazilian youths, with the practice of the academic pillage, the habit of the "exam-cheating", while working as great first and widespread training form for that way of life.

It is necessary with urgency, through school and communication media, to value the dignity, the aggregated economical earnings and the therapeutic power of the manual labor.

Numbers. Psychologically, do Brazilians appreciate numbers?

Before the construction of the defect of the Ergophobia, Brazilians received as inheritance the Arithmophobia, horror to the use of the Hindu-Arabic numerals.

It is well known that this problem came from Portugal and there is no innovation here in repeating the statement. The same Arabs who inspired in a direct way and helped Infant Don Henry to set up the School of Sagres and to leverage the country for the exploration of the seas, in an indirect way they implanted in the Portuguese lands the rejection to the cultivation of the numeric calculations.

The information that is probably new to the reader gives account that this rejection to the numbers was built by reverse effect.

Along five centuries, from 711 to 1249, time that the Arab occupation of the Iberian Peninsula lasted, the Portuguese, joined to the Spaniards, developed a fight much less physics than cultural against that dominance. This consisted of rejecting many items of the culture that Arabs brought. Although the language has been very flooded of Arabic expressions, the names of people, the ciphers and other characteristics of those settlers were badly seen. The common people didn't know that the ciphers were Hindu, and then they rejected them as one of the worst things brought by the Islamic.

Latin America, finally, received this load of rejection, very located. There is no prejudice against Arab in Brazil, being enough to see the proportion of elected politicians who have this origin. But the resistance to the ciphers, a safe source of underdevelopment, reaches enormous portion of Latin-American people. In the soul of each one, it is as if it was reason of pride to maintain this "ideological" line of the Portuguese or Spanish settler. So much that Julio Cesar de Mello e Souza (1895-1974), when decided to write his books of popularization of history of the arithmetic in Brazil and other countries of Latin America, noticed that with Portuguese name he would not have chance of going very far. He created a pseudonym then, Malba Tahan, to speak of an Arab character skilled in doing calculations. He became success of sales, while indicating that it came to fill out an immense gap of the culture of the subcontinent.

To abolish the horror to the numbers, the Mathematics teachers, with the support of the governments, need to use artifices, as Malba Tahan made, and to transform themselves in enthusiastic advertisers of the marvels of this science, not just instructors of its techniques.

Extravagant. Do the behavioral defects of Brazilians get complete here?

Certainly the defects above are not just the only ones that Brazilians carry, for tradition. But almost all the other identifiable defects fit in those ten. For instance, the habit of deceiting line, not the physician line, because almost nobody likes to be hit, but the virtual line, how to pay medical agreement with the intention of being called first at the public hospital of high level. Other defects are really extravagant, as the one of stealing for the State. Everybody knows that to steal from the State is corruption, a thing of criminals. But there is also the habit of stealing from the citizen, mainly the humbler public employee, to transfer the earnings to the State. An example is this of forcing the servant to work more time than that legally foreseen. An emblematic case is that of a friend of the author who decided to cancel the labor agreement in a public university. They brought the fine so that he paid, with mockery air, while thinking he would not get it. But his wife sold an apartment received in inheritance and she lent all the money for the payment of that fine. The ones who make that type of subtraction are insane delinquent, because the State is a cold machine (Max Weber), which doesn't reward the flatterer. Who has difficulty in understanding the coldness of the State machine, think about the two centuries of guillotinements in France.

As well as one should not accept the practice of stealing from the citizen to favor the State, either it sounds plausible to work "by grace" for the State. Who wants to be Good Samaritan, should help his brother, natural person, not the machine. The two larger cases of corruption (up to 2014) in Brazil, in 1992 and in 2006, were played by two citizens who, in practice, rendered service without remuneration. The first died murdered, while the second was condemned to forty years of seclusion.

Working "by grace" for the State almost always involves some excuse objective and for this it is a practice that should be banned categorically. Municipal counselors, for instance, should receive payment for their work, at least as "jeton", i. e., for session. Also the situation in that somebody wants to remunerate of the own pocket the expense that should be public should be banned. What Michael Bloomberg did as mayor of New York in his three continued periods, while paying from the own pocket official trips and several other expenses of the city hall, can seem a citizen action, but it is the opposite. He gave a bad example, maybe with the best of the intentions.

Prejudices. Have the negative discriminations been increasing in Brazil?

We cannot also let to pass without mention the subject of the ethnic and socioeconomic prejudices. The racism in Brazil was hidden, almost always veiled. With the penetration of TV in the popular classes, while bringing its programs from the United States, the color prejudice in Brazil came to be less and less veiled, more and more explicit, even with the Afonso Arinos Law, which punishes the racist attitude and was incorporated in the Constitution of 1988. And it is good to notice that capital crime of racism, crime of racial feeling, cannot exist, but just crime of racist manifestation. And this is what comes increasing, besides receiving reinforcement on the part of the possible victims, instigated by influential people, but colonized mind. As for the social discrimination, it is something more noticed by the foreigners who visit Brazil. Books of business tactics, written in the United States, teach the foreign investor to work in Brazil while showing the psychological characteristics of the country. The first point that those books treat is the enormous discrimination of social class, joined to the great disparity of income between the richest and the poorest, phenomenon to what French Andre Gorz denominated "Brazilization". A country with such a discrepancy is a divided house. If Brazilians insist on maintaining this situation, it won't form a country of brothers, but a resentful one. The education cannot be "ideological", one that maintains the poor in the poverty. It needs to be pro human being, promoter of the humble ones, for turning itself into instrument of social mobility, not of enchasement.

6. On structures

Parties. Does the organization of the political parties in Brazil need correction?

Brazil never lived under a unique party, and will probably never live. This is part of the half anarchical soul of the Brazilians, who reject, for this, the simple mention to pass some period submitted to retreat, as the dictatorships make world out. In the monarchic time, the government was disputed by two parties, the liberal and the conservative. With the coming of the Republic many parties went being created, until that the military regime, established on April 15, 1964, dissolved all of them and opened space for the formation of only two, which came to be the National Renovating Alliance (Arena), to support the coup activists, and the Brazilian Democratic Movement (MDB), to do what was called at that time "consented opposition".

Still inside the Figueiredo government, last of the military regime, one extinguished the prohibition of formation of new parties, and then the Party of the Workers (PT) and the Brazilian Labor Party (PTB) appeared, both in 1980. As the PTB resurged in bases eminently conservatives, from the hands of Representative Ivete Vargas, niece of Getulio Vargas, Leonel Brizola founded the Democratic Labor Party (PDT), which obtained registration in 1981. The PT and the PDT appeared basically as dissidence of the MDB, but on the PTB we cannot say the same. One of the first affiliated came to be the great opponent of the old PTB, Janio Quadros.

With the New Republic, in 1985, new parties were being created, while reaching the number of 32 in the year of 2013.

The specialists of politics know that the proportional system of parliamentary voting tends to do to increase the number of parties, while the old majority district vote restricts the amount. But the Brazilians notice that the great profusion of created parties has not been good for the political health of the country and they shout for some measure that reduces the existent number.

Years ago one tried the acting clause, which would impose a minimum of chairs obtained for the party to guarantee representation in the Federal Camera. Nine years after having been approved, the measure was dropped in the Federal Supreme Court, under the frightening allegation that the restriction would attempt against the freedom of expression. Although many politicians dream in retaking this path, it was dynamited. It is necessary to look for new exits.

Instead of imposing a minimum number of chairs, it can be made the demand of number of States, for instance. Party that does not elect representatives in at least three unities of the federation, gets without chairs. When repeating this in the following election, it loses the registration. It also suits, with the largest possible urgency, that one eliminates the mechanism of the coalitions for proportional elections, what allows minuscule parties to choose representatives in the vacuum of the votes of the big parties. And parties with religious names should be prohibited, because the mixture State-religion is the most dangerous form of demagogy.

Another measure that can be taken is the determination that each one of the parties uses one of the three primary colors (of Maxwell), blue, red or green. These colors can represent three of the four Aristotelian cardinal virtues, which are the moderation, the justice and the prudence. The fortress, fourth virtue, is in the hands of the armed forces, not of the parties. Since then one takes measures that motivate the coalition of the parties of a same color. Finally, the number of each party is reduced to a single digit, what should traverse the scale from 1 to 9, once nobody will want his party has the digit zero. If the maximum number of parties is restricted to nine, Brazilians will have very more clarity of the proposals of each one, and the politicians themselves will know how to take place doctrinally while having to work with a small number of associations.

Today (2014) there is, for instance, only two heavy conservative parties, which are PP and PTB, supported by two miniparties, PRTB and PTC. As liberal parties, DEM, PR, PSD, PRB and one more quartet of smaller acronyms can be counted. Others locate themselves in the social-democratic spectrum, of center-left, like PMDB, PT, PSDB, PSB, PV, PDT, PCdoB and PPS, being classified in the left PSOL, PCO, PPL, PCB and PSTU. The other ones are satellites of the center-left parties.

The classic liberals, who have fright of the possible situation of falling in only party, don't need to have this concern in mind, because the antidote was created right here in South America. If the number of parties shrinks for one or two, after restriction measures, the mechanism of the sub-lemmas is applied (Luis Vicente Varela, Paris, 1875). Each party that remains is automatically divided in three currents, or sub-lemmas, for effect of campaign and proportionality of chairs. The institute of the proportional vote itself demands this.

If the parties that feel of left, and also the teachers of the same condition, understand that is necessary to explain to the youth as for the difference between fascism and right wingism, those same parties and teachers need to admit that to renounce the idea of competition means to work for the worst competition type. They should understand that the only alternative to the sound competition is the rude competition of the natural selection. The first type involves learning, cooperation, transparency and mobility, while the second only accepts dominance and slaughter. He who looks for a third option is concealing the first and, therefore, is giving the youth to the wild animal of the second one.

Ministries. For the good administration, is the amount of ministries indifferent?

The increase of the number of ministries, through the growth of the demagogy, is symptom of deterioration of the politics. When Sarkozy took oath as president of France in 1990, there were 62. He promised to reduce that amount, and it fell for fifteen. In Somalia, after the anomie period, between 1993 and 2000, the government was redone and the amount was approximately the same than in France. A great administrator, premier Prof. Ali Khalif Galaydh, who governed during the year of 2001, reduced the number of ministries for eighteen.

Those numbers, fifteen, eighteen, or any other close to this, are good numbers, but they have something of arbitrary and are changed by the following governments again, sooner or later. The ideal is to fasten in a dozen the maximum number of organs, or, better still, in ten. Even so, Argentina, that had ten as limiting number, now (in 2014) is with fifteen ministries (it is not possible to hold the deforming power of the demagogy).

The ten necessary ministries should be:
1. Finance-planning
2. Industry-energy
3. Civil House - science
4. Transport-communications
5. Foreign Relationships
6. Education-culture
7. Justice-work
8. Agriculture-cattle
9. Defense-environment
10. Health-welfare

They are the ten fingers of the hand and the ten colors of the electronics, besides the ten Aristotelian categories. In those ten organs all of the activities of the government can be contained. In the case of the provincial or municipal governments, the area of External Relationships can be substituted by Public Political or Institutional Relationships. In the national government, the agencies, the autarchies, the public banks and any organs of the administration are subordinated to the ministries. Instead of three or four ministries to take care of a same area, as it happens today with the Justice, the Foreign Relationships and the Agriculture, a single ministry takes care of all of the correlate activities. In the Ministry of the Industry, for instance, besides the Energy, the general offices of Trade, Tourism, Show-business, Professional Sports and Mines can be included. In the Civil House, besides Science, one can include Technology, Administration and Institutional Relationships. And the title-holder of this Ministry is the premier, who accumulates the position of presidential spokesperson. In the Ministry of the Justice one can join Work, Job, Cities, Interior, Safety, Woman, Promotion of Minorities and National Integration. In the Agriculture should be Cattle, Fishes, Agrarian Development, Estate Politics and Irrigation. The Ministry of Health, besides the general office of the Social Welfare and others, also joins the general office of the Puericulture, to take care of the Preschool Education (children of zero to five years old), which is not instruction, but "nursery", i. e., child care, subject of health, not of the Ministry of Education.

In the distribution of the ministries, the care should be had for vesting five ministers coming of the area of exact sciences and technology (technical elite), and other five of the area of biomedical sciences and humanities (classical elite). So we have the bipartite administration, which incorporates the modernity there.

Yes, it is difficult to do businesses with parties for constitution of allied base with a reduced number of ministries. But the big number, as much of parties as of ministries, serves before everything to transform the government in hostage of opportunists and climbers.

Transition. How can the country, without traumas, become parliamentarist?

How the country wants that the government has a prime-minister, some measures could be taken, in a slow way, to arrive to the Soft Parliamentarism, a form of parliamentarism that preserves the positive aspects of what was built as presidentialism. The mechanism is adjusted to what the Constitution foresaw in its initial elaboration and serves as prevention against future political crises. The steps should be the followings.

A) The minister-chief of the Civil House is the first to be indicated by the president.
B) The minister-chief aids the president to fill out the other ministries.
C) The minister-chief becomes called prime minister, or premier.
D) The premier accumulates position of presidential spokesperson, to win exhibition.
E) The premier is member of the party with more chairs in the Camera in the oath day.

If tie happens among the parties with more chairs in the Camera, the Electoral Superior Court decides the election in favor of the party that has more chairs in most populous Federal Unity. In this case, that party wins a new chair for this same Unity, in disfavor of the party with smaller number of chairs, which loses this chair that would be the arduously conquered, even if it is only one. If somebody finds strange that the president has to vest as minister-chief somebody of the party with more chairs, independently of the composition of the Camera, he should notice that this is the alternative to the old crooked deals to what the president has to give to set up the government in the effective presidentialism until this beginning of millennium.

When vesting the minister-chief, who becomes the premier, the President indicates a first and a second vice prime ministers, who won't be paid in this function of waiting.

Executive. Are there many changes to implement in the performance of the ministries?

In each area there is a group of actions that should orientate a project of developed country, once guaranteed the end of the larger bottleneck. In the economy, managed by the Ministry of Finance and the Central Bank, it is necessary to guarantee liquidity and low of interests, inside sound limits, with credit warranty to the recently formed entrepreneurs, and always to promote a favorable exchange politics to the exporter. The tax burden should be rationalized, with substantial reductions, being avoided exemptions, allied to a strategy of severe combat to the withholding and the corruption. The progressive tax rates should be forbidden gradually in all of the instances of government, with the attendance of a permanent work of reinforcement in the teaching of the theory of the proportions in the school unities starting from the gymnasium level, so that the economical agents understand and support the application of the proportional tributes. The legal entities, of all of the types, should collect monthly in specific bill in the bank 1/24 of the conceited income tax for the year in subject. In the Ministry of the Industry educational campaigns should be released, always renewed, of service to tourists. Laws should guarantee the interiorization of the industrialization, being avoided the concentric cycles in the metropolitan areas, and for these new factories are permitted just along highways and railways, at a distance never larger than 500 m. New sources of energy should be researched and, if possible, implemented and the investments should increase in the transmission lines starting from the hydroelectrics. Patents of inventions and models of usefulness should receive financing, or even parceling of payments, and the significant innovations should receive prizes, in annual editions.

The Ministry of the *Civil* House and Science need to implement an efficient plan of abolition of the culture of the waste, without that it can mean abandonment of the superfluous ones, for not falling in the Mandeville's "Fable of the Bees". The giving without compensation ('datio') needs to be discussed and seen as dangerous thing to the government and to the future of the population. The positions of trust should have limiting number fastened in law. The teachers, in the schools, and the doctors and paramedical, in the hospitals, direct their institutions again, with warranty of prohibition of courses that form professional bureaucrats for the leadership positions in those organs, namely, school administration and hospital administration. The central objective of the government should be the permanent elevation of HDI of Municipal districts and States. One should publish every month of December in bilingual edition, English and homeland language, the Annual of the Science, with abstracts of the notable researches, and the development of the passion for the science in the youths' mind needs to dominate the concern of the rulers.

The Ministry of *Transports*, which absorbs the areas of Communications and Telecommunications, should invest heavily in the revitalization and construction of railways and hydroways. And one should prohibit dubbing in TV out of infantile programs, so that the population leaves the glass dome of the complacency of not reading, at least legends. Programs on crimes should only be allowed at night, starting from 23 h.

The Ministry of *Foreign* Relationships needs to struggle for the return of the teaching of Portuguese language in Goa, India, because the youths of this area no longer speak the language that belonged to their parents. The same should be made in relation to Macao. It should also abandon the insistence in doing with that the rich countries stop subsidizing their farmers and abandoning the search for a permanent chair in the Security Council of the United Nations. If the practice of Brazil is to abstain in the votings, what grace there is in getting this chair? Besides, why to embrace this cause, without knowing if the country is viable?

The Ministry of *Education* will have arduous work after the removal of the bottleneck, if it happens. It is necessary to prohibit graduations in Pedagogy and in Superior Normal, substituting all this for the graduation in Psychology of Education, a course mounted in scientific bases, with the subject matters Statistics and Laboratory of Psychology. The education degrees need to be abolished, being introduced the subject-matter General Psychology in all of the baccalaureates, because the necessary general knowledge for the teaching is the one of the Psychology. The materials that lately are freely distributed at schools for the child are, in the way in which the thing is made, a misfortune for the trade, because it tramples it and kills it. All material to be supplied, from blouse to pencil, going by notebooks and books, should be given in the form of tickets, to the parents' hand, never to the little students, so that those parents change them in the stores. And the books cannot have edition differentiated in relation to those sold to private schools. After the release of the program of books of the medium teaching, the closing of bookstores in Brazil became epidemic. This in a country lacking of stores of books. As for the scholarships, they should not be of the same value for students accomplishing of the study obligations and those who just warm up the school seats. Starting from a basic value, the payment should receive increment relatively to the good performance of the student. Otherwise, the sign that the ministry gives to the schools is that the "frolic" should be rewarded, so much when the dedication.

As for the contents, Physics should be the subject-matter more valued and protected in the medium teaching, and in the gymnasium level as independent subject-matters the Geometric Drawing, the Music and the Manual Works should return. Teachers of the official teaching, as well as any professionals of superior level in the public service, who maintain their smaller children in the official schools, without using private net, should receive salary incentive for this, at least a monthly bonus of 2%, the son-bonus, benefit that extinguishes when the servant doesn't have more minor children in the net. And the hour is almost passed for beginning the preparation of the abolition of the presence of the teacher in the elementary three-year period, of the children from six to eight years old, according to scientific discovery of Maria Montessori. Those children should be taken care by students' inspectors, and the traditional role of the teacher stops being to accompany them in the room and become the one of examiner, who prepares tasks, evaluations and corrections, without entering class. With role similar to teacher, one opens up exception just for the music instructor, who should enter class, one hour a week when a lot, to teach ballads for literacy and other songs, including also those in foreign language. This system should begin in pilot-unity, to enlarge as soon as the results show superiors to that of the traditional model. In the remaining of the basic teaching, the presence of the teachers in class, with the students, should never cross the daily period of 5 h. In the higher education, the ministry should work so that in the future the only specific diplomas obligatory by law come to be the ones of Medical Surgeon and Dentist Surgeon.

The Ministry of *Justice*, which incorporates the general offices of Work, Safety, Interior and others, has several incumbencies in the task of unlocking the paths of the country. The first is to abolish the "industry of the injunction". A judicial injunction becomes just accepted if signed by two judges, of different districts when they are judges of first instance. In the Federal Supreme Court (STF), Tuesdays should be reserved to the dispute relative to the public service, while passing to other cases when there is not process of public service in the line. To the document of national identity, "nationalized ID", it is enough the added state numbers of the acronym of the federal unity to be used, for instance, somebody of Sao Paulo, with number 5.731.914-5, starts to have his identity number added of SP soon after the verification digit: 005.731.914-5-SP. It is not necessary to do any revolution in the numbering of identification of the Brazilians. The maximum penalty should be changed urgently of 30 years for 50 years, once the interpretation on the benefit of the penalty reduction destroyed the original spirit of the proposal of Armando Falcao and the criminals are loosened very much before the time, many of them coming to kill the judges who condemned them.

Still in the extent of the Justice, it urges to repair the Law of Auction, with views to eliminate the "industry of the fraudulent auction". They are only two the necessary mechanisms: (a) who petitions in the justice process for annulment of result is impeded of competing to following rounds of the auction in subject and (b) company that wins auction is forbidden of subcontracting losers.

In the extent of the Work, one should institute that the trade-union presidency should be of one year, without right to reelection; one should substitute "dismissal of employees'" for "compulsory transfer", in that the employee discarded of the company is transferred for another company or for a public organ responsible for his relocating in the job market, without there being the commitment that his following wage is not smaller than the previous; one should demand that the registration in wallet includes, besides the direct wage, the roll, with values, of all of the indirect wages to what the employee has right; one should demand that great companies offer vacancies for minor apprentices, and the fourteen years old minimum age should be lowered for thirteen; one should guarantee that the employer is released of paying responsibilities while his employee renders military service; one should build gradually the era of the full employment, which implicates control in politics of immigration and birth rate; one should legally impede the programmed stoppage of public service, even of concessionaire (public servant doesn't make strike, he makes lockout) and one should continue guaranteeing the stability of the public servant in the position, not in the work place.

As for the area of Safety, one should prohibit sale retail of distilled alcoholic drink; the trade of narcotics should be instituted for hospitals and universities (B2B), while staying prohibition for natural person; the inconsistent "abating law" should be revoked and one should determine that all fallow public land in the urban area becomes park. The Ministry should also collect the abandonment of the fascist regional division of IBGE (Brazilian Institute of Geography and Statistic) implanted in 1970, which created this frightened entity called Southeast Region, and to demand the return of the historical-cultural regional division as it consisted of the Atlas-Mec of 1963, of the Darcy Ribeiro administration, in that Sao Paulo belongs to the South Region.

For the Ministry of *Agriculture*, the tasks are to turn exclusive for agriculture the strip of width 20 km in the whole border extension, except in the passages in that there is natural impediment; to determine that in the Amazonian area the properties are impeded of dropping strips of more than 30 m of forest, while having to alternate 30 m of forest and 30 m of cultivation; it suits to impede that lands are donated in the field (to avoid mortal conflicts), while guaranteeing that every acquisition is made by inheritance or for purchase, with facilitation of mortgages, in action of citizenship, not of guardianship; it suits to work so that every Northeastern city of the polygon of the droughts has its weir-dam, in way to no more to suffer for lack of water; it suits to guarantee regulator stock with priority in the purchases to the small producer and to invest in research of fruits and grains of high protein tenor.

Of the Ministry of *Defense*, which incorporates the general office of Environment, for the conclusion of the Northern Perimetral Highway is waited, as ecological highway; the surveys of most of the Amazonian forest still live and the calling to the military service of all of the sixteen years old youths who continue illiterate, without exception, with views to alphabetize them in the barracks. For this, the selection is instituted for all at the sixteen years old, summoning the literate selected one to present at the eighteen years old. Those sixteen years old who are illiterate are summoned immediately for the installment of the military service, for two years, in this case. The father who not to agree has annulled his family power on the minor, who passes to the guardianship of the commandant of the military detachment to what he will serve. The alternative would be to lower the civil majority of the illiterate, but this should not be made, so that it is not signaled support to the reduction of the penal age. Unlike what the conservatives think, the minor ones need help, on those times in that they are fed with all of the types of data, which are to delay their matureness, not to accelerate it, once datum is not information.

Finally, the Ministry of *Health*, which incorporates Social Welfare and Puericulture, takes care of publishing a Phytoterapic Magazine, annual, to be distributed in the Basic Units of Health, and of reviewing the politics of childbirths, while attributing priorities to the obstetrician doctor and the obstetrician nurse, and to the traditional midwives and doulas, not to the common doctor. It also takes care of prohibiting psychotropics to minor of eighteen years old. In relation to the Welfare, it is urgent that it separates the social security fund of the other benefits, and he should go by annual auditing.

Parliament. What will be the paths to improve the image of the parliament?

With the institution of the Soft Parliamentarism, the National Congress strengthens a lot, while becoming more respected by the population. But it is necessary to adopt many other ways to improve the image of the representatives of the population.

1. Minute of the Congress in TV (1 week min - one reduces Voice of Brazil in the radio).
2. Parliamentary of the Year Award, by pairs, to the author of the best revocatory law.
3. Popularization at each year-end of classification of most frequent parliamentarians.
4. Withholding only to judicially condemned, never withholding by lack of decency.
5. Substitute of Senator is the more senior federal deputy of the bench.
6. Norm: in presidency of City Council, woman succeeds man and vice versa.

7. Priority in the candidacies to the retired ones - after parliamentarians with mandate.
8. Temporary Measure just in first useful day of the semester (or those "very urging").
9. Annual seminars in the Interlegis on Malthus, Keynes and Schumpeter.
10. Writing Elementary Exam of Grammar and Mathematics for candidates (beginners).
11. Exhibition of the marks in the exam of Grammar and Math in the electoral schedule.
12. Reforms in the Constitution only voted for of ten in ten years - in the years of end 1.

Another important care is that the Commission of Constitution and Justice needs to enlarge its incumbencies, as way of increasing the credibility of the parliament. Before the projects that are approved and liberated for the plenary session or for the following commissions, they should go to public audience, after having released to the press, with the objective of discussing their pertinence and opportunity. Ridiculous, innocuous, noxious and discriminatory projects should be discarded, with the help of the civil society.

The hour is almost passed so that the parliament guards against the pendant projects of opportunist representatives, the called "smuggling of projects". Somebody that tries to push an inappropriate law and doesn't get it, couples it as smuggling of a pertinent project and, by incautiousness of most, he approves his Trojan Horse. For instance, whenever some parliamentary tries to legalize the zoo animal game, another one mends the project with the legalization of the casinos. Michel Temer, when president of the Camera, took measures against the smuggling in Temporary Measures, but the one of common projects continue to threaten the country.

Conservatism. Is it possible to identify the true conservatives starting from their ideas?

Each time has its cave, formed by a group of faiths that are believed the state of the art, but that are pure "ideology", in the original sense of the word, which is the one of mental confusion.

In the last times, it is common among the youths to attack the progress of the Catholic Church, conquered after 1965, when of the conclusion of the Second Vatican Council, as being a conservative agenda, without noticing the fact, and without ones open their eyes for it, that conservative was the politics of the Hitlerist times, which tolerated and even cultivated the forms of programmed death that the State of that time implemented (a little before being in force the new Church, the immense majority of the clergy supported the coup of 1964 in Brazil).

With this, the true conservative thought passes as an innocent thing, and even acceptable, for the great portion of youth. It is never too much, therefore, to present the more central points of this politics, which are not the one of the citizens who conserve good things, as some judge to believe, but the one of the ones who defend the saddest practices of the human history. Churchill was in the Conservative Party as well as Severo Gomes was in the Arena, parties of the status quo, but they were not examples of conservative people. Conservatives were Meletus, Commodus and Filinto Muller. The points that identify them in the days today go below.

    A) *Politics*. Guaranteeing majority, volunteer and district (or mixed) vote.
    B) *Economy*. Assuring *laissez-faire* for the employment.
    C) *Government*. Promoting privatization of the public services.
    D) *Promotion*. Maintaining a breed of donors of alms.
    E) *Society*. Cultivating contempt to the social responsibility of the companies.
    F) *Safety*. Instituting municipal police.
    G) *Justice*. Supporting capital punishment.

Of course the citizen can be follower of one or two of those points without joining the traditional conservatives. But, anyway, it will be a preoccupying sign.

The district vote was already discussed above, but there are still other aspects of this subject, as the minimum age. To the first view, lowering the minimum age seems thing of advanced people. It is not. Who lowered from eighteen to sixteen years old this age in the Constitution was a politician of the PTB. The game is to argue after the penal age should also be lowered. Now, who votes for can be voted for, therefore, the minimum age should be fastened in 21 years old.

And as for the unemployment? It is not more reasonable than this exists, after so much time passed from John Maynard Keynes death. As the message of that economist was not published with honesty, what was an exigency that he always did, the world attends the creation of lids that are to move away for far away the arrival of the system of full employment. The "food stamps" (feeding cards, implanted by the Franklin Delano Roosevelt government) and the unemployment insurance are examples of this. The government owes, yes, to supply feeding, but only for the disable persons, according to Thomas Robert Malthus proposal. For the others, it should provide job, having this been the purpose of Keynes in his entire academic work. The unemployment insurance seems something good, but it can only be considered as good thing before the sabotage that ones did to the Keynesian ideas, which are not summarized to the proposal of the government intervention in the moments of economical crisis. The proposal is government politics that guarantees full employment. Conservatives want the *laissez-faire*, the illusion of the Say's Law (everything that is produced, one sells; this assumed law was one more fruit of the old confusion between antecedent and consequent, between necessary condition and enough condition: everything that is sold is because it was in offer, and not the opposite).

As for the privatization of the public services, this is another defense that seems advanced thing. But it incorporates at least two traps against the progress: it implicates "robbing" entrepreneurs of the production to bring them to the public service, which should be the incumbency of the government, and it also implicates to bring damages to people who belong to some prejudiced category by the demand of "good look", people who are employed easily in the public service, through contests that don't take into account the color of the eyes, but who get without the correspondents work vacancies in the private services.

The breed of donors of alms is quite necessary in the view of conservatives, because in their politics should not there are jobs for all and, so, many will fall in poverty situation, while becoming dependent of charitable people who sustain them, once the government should not be assigned of this. Likewise, the social responsibility of the companies, which is an exigency of the progressive lines of the academy, should not be cultivated. For the conservative, one should give to the companies absolute freedom, without any imposition besides the tributes.

Finally, in relation to safety and justice, the deterioration of the human behavior is always seen as moral problem, without concerning with objective conditions, while being, therefore, the death penalty a good instrument of solution of the social problems, always according to the conservatives. And, in their understanding, for there being more effectiveness in the application of the repression on the criminals, even if is not possible to guarantee the death penalty, the police has to be municipal, present in all of the moments and maintained under responsibility of the local power.

These are the more central aspects of the conservatives' action today.

Greatness. With the positive programs above, is not guaranteed the viability of Brazil?

Unhappily, or maybe even happily, there is not the path to make possible Brazil as a political entity. There are five crystallized bottlenecks, whose combined removal is not in the horizon of the probable things.

A) Brasilia as presidential residence - Ravenna Effect.
B) Presidential direct election - apple of the eyes of the Messianic populism.
C) Fascist regional division, of 1970, with its Southeast Region.
D) Horror to the Culture of the Merit and to the autochthonous innovation.
E) Rejection to the entity Brazil by the unconscious - what induced Brasilia and presidential direct election.

Brasilia appeared by upstart impulse of a chief of State slashed for that moment. He had only to accomplish a plan designed long time ago in the dreamlike area of the minds, as a nightmare that made to advance as a dream of glory.

The presidential direct election came from reverse effect against the military regime. If the military ones had given two presents to Brazil, the taken of Brasilia already in 1960 and the adoption of presidential direct election ever since, by reverse effect Brazilians would have moved away the two disasters in 1985: they would have returned the presidential residence to Rio and would have abolished the presidential direct election. But the viability of the country was not drawn in the unconscious of the humanity.

The solution is in a different plan. The path is to dilute the country in South America. This doesn't mean to give up the history, the culture and the unit of heart of the Brazilian people. On the contrary, this means to strengthen stiller this perspective, with the help of the brother countries of the area, also offering to them, by synergy, opportunity of united growth.

In the beginning of 2014, seven Brazilian parties counted with more than a million affiliated: PMDB (2,36 million), PT (1,59), PP (1,42), PSDB (1,35), PDT (1,21), PTB (1,19) and DEM (1,09). Of these, at least the first four ones need to embrace with enthusiasm the cause of the South American integration, as delineated below, mainly the largest among them, PMDB. It was in the Sarney government, PMDB, that the integration has had beginning in fact.

One cannot count on the structure of the Una-Sur (Union of the Nations of the South), which is an entity built by the Bolivarian rulers, but little functional. Nor on the old Group of Rio (G-Rio), uniting Latin America and Caribbean, which the Bolivarians changed for Celac (Community of States of Latin America and Caribbean) and that is presided now by Raul Castro. The base of the super-federation is the Merco-Sur (Common Market of the South: without hyphen, the pronunciation in Portuguese would have to be "mercozul"). In fact, the ugliness of this impure acronym, Merco-Sur, is a great reason to leave back the present phase of the relationships among States of South America.

If the Merco-Sur incorporates Bolivia, it will have area of 13,889,765 km², smaller just than the one of Russia, among the countries. This federation becomes the fifth country of the world in nominal GDP, with 3,461,465,000 of North American dollars, in values of 2011, while being behind only of Germany, Japan, China and USA (being taken into account that the European Union still doesn't come as a country). With the future entrance of Colombia, it passes to the fourth position, above Germany.

The Merco-Sur, which should pass to be called Union of South America, has all of the possible proximities to already turn a single country. It is the Leviathan Process, in that each member State delivers power, for reaching a larger power. Below we see how making possible the new stage.

A) *Term*. The presidency of the Union of South America should be exercised under biannual mandate, without re-conduction, with the oath of the title-holder always in January, 2, of the even years. In the action of the oath, the President cancels affiliating of any party to what he is linked. The next President can already exercise the mandate during the present even-odd biennium.

B) *Presidency*. The President of the block should be a prominent figure, internationally recognized, at least 50 years old, chosen by the presidents of the member States of the Union: when Argentinean, he can be somebody as Quino; when Brazilian, somebody like Pelé. After five presidents, i. e., after ten years, the demand of a name of international expression won't be so more relevant. The chosen name needs to be countersigned and vested by the Parliament of the Merco-Sur, the Parlia-Sur.

C) *Residence*. The Presidents of the block should live in the fixed capital, the presidential capital, during the biennium of the mandate, and this capital is Rio de Janeiro (*"conditio sine qua non"*, to avoid the horrible Versailles-Weimar Effect - other city can give worse result than Brussels). The presidential capital should always be Rio - saving Rio, destroyed by the Juscelinist abandonment, is to save Latin America. We have to avoid always the three motors of the historical tragedy: capitalnewism, lifelongness and theocracy.

D) *Geography*. The presidency of the federation is occupied by Lusophones, of the five Brazilian people (they become the republic-regions of Pinegroves-South - RS to SP -, Atlantic-East - RJ to SE -, Palms-Northeast - AL to MA -, Amazonian-North - TO to AC -, Savannah-West - RO to GO-DF -, While having as honorary presidents the governors of the federal unities of the main capitals, which are, respectively, Sao Paulo, Rio, Fortaleza, Manaus and Brasilia - the base is the historical-cultural regional division, not the one of the military government, of 1970, and those governors become presidents of the development superintendence, Sudene, Sudam, Sudeco, Sudessul and Sudeleste), and Hispanic, of States of the Southest-Cone and Andes, by the alphabetical order: Amazonian, Argentina, Atlantic, Bolivia (after entering), Savannah, Palms, Paraguay, Pinegroves, Uruguay, Venezuela. (The Hispanic members can present resistance to the idea of occupying the presidency in this way, but a simple rota among the current countries, as occurs today, weakens the block and practically makes it unfeasible, because of the weight of Brazil, which, for this, needs to be fractionated in the five republics - the Constitution of Brazil forbids the end of the federation, but not a redivision.)

E) *Commission*. The parliament and the administration (Executive Commission) should move of Montevideo to Buenos Aires - maintaining those organs in Uruguay means to remove of Argentina the motivation to participate in the block.

F) *Premier*. The Parlia-Sur chooses the minister-chief, president of the Executive Commission in Buenos Aires, with four-year term, without immediate re-conduction, while being able to come back to the position after eight years out of it. The Executive Commission works with ten organs (ministries), as maximum number (Finance, Industry, Science, Transport-communication, Foreign Relationships, Education, Justice-work, Agriculture, Defense-environment, Health-welfare).

G) *Capital*. The Central Bank is settled in Montevideo (financial capital), the Supreme Court in Caracas (judiciary capital), the School of Polytechnic Engineering of the Army in Assumption (strategic capital), cities that will account to Buenos Aires (administrative capital) and Rio de Janeiro (political capital). The Union doesn't adopt Constitution, but just the Electoral Law and the habitual codes (civil, penal, tax,...).

H) *Currency*. The common currency should be created, while working in the first years in scriptural form, not coined. It should be taken into account the brief life of coin called by trisyllable, as "peseta" or "escudo".

I) *Balance*. In all of the mandates, five title-holders, among the ten ministries, should belong to the technical elite (professionals of engineering, computation or exact sciences) and other five ones should be of the classical elite (professionals of biomedical sciences or humanities). The Carly Fiorina Effect is avoided.

J) *Structure*. Close to the presidency in Rio one should create (a) a small presidential guard - formed by members of the armed forces of the member States -, (b) an agency of news with a producing of radio-TV and internet and (c) a daily video-conference system connected with the administration in Buenos Aires. A biannual presidency exercised in the fastened presidential capital (Rio) will bring the definitive consolidation of the federation, while recruiting respect and recognition on the part of the people of the jurisdiction. On first Sunday of every semester the president talks in chain of radio-TV about the political-economical situation of the block (if in Spanish, with subscripts in Portuguese; if in Portuguese, with subscripts in Spanish). Brazil, with its five people, commits to introduce the subject-matter Spanish Language in the last year of the fundamental teaching, ninth grade, because the official languages of the Union of South America should be (1) Spanish, (2) Portuguese and (3) Tupi-Guarani - hereafter, also English, because of Guyana. On safety, the member States commit to prohibit trade and load of weapons of short pipe (light weapons or short guns). The differences of economical level, as this existent between Bolivia and Argentina, will be overcome much more quickly in the new political geography. With the time, the South Americans of the Pacific Ocean will start to participate in the federation.

It suits to repeat that the *"conditio sine qua non"* for the operation of the federation, and of the consequent viability of the continent, in the direction of the conquest of the South American population's happiness, is the installation of the presidential residence in Rio de Janeiro. Being disposed (i) the president in Rio de Janeiro and (ii) the chief of the Executive Commission (premier) in Buenos Aires, one creates the necessary sharing that will make the South American brother people live really as siblings. For this, one cannot neglect (iii) the regional division of Brazil, which should not be the one of the fascism, of 1970. It is also very important, for the warranty of progress, that (iv) the ministries are distributed half for professionals of exact sciences and technology and other half for professionals of biological sciences and humanities. Finally, (v) the president of the Union, it suits to stress, has two-year term, without re-conduction. And the regional demagogy becomes neutralized by the central power, built on strategic foundations, rid from the populism that has been diving in the mediocrity and in the absence of perspectives the Latin-American populations in general.

@cacildo
cacildomarques@gmail.com